The Book of Revelation Devotional

Your Journey through the Book of Revelation

A 366-day devotional

The Revelation Devotional

Cover illustration:
Front cover illustration: The Open Door in Heaven (Revelation 4:1)
Back cover illustration: The City Four-square; New Jerusalem (Revelation 21:1-21)

Artwork by Pat Marvenko Smith, ©1982/1992
www.revelationillustrated.com

Jacket design: Sean Flanagan
Edited by: Leslie L. McKee

Formatting by: Rik at Wild Seas Formatting

Published by: Jule Inc.
Peoria, Illinois
PO Box 10705
Peoria, Illinois 61612

andyzach.net/jeffryjsmith/
jeffryjsmith@andyzach.net

Library of Congress Control Number: 2023922951
ISBN: 978-1-959962-01-4

Published in the United States of America

Copyright Page Contents

The Zondervan Parallel New Testament in Greek and English
The Nestle's Greek New Testament by Eberhard Nestle
The King James Version
The New International Version

Grateful acknowledgment is given to BibleGateway.com for the use of their website, which made accessing the numerous Bible versions I used easy and user-friendly. These are the translations I used or consulted in this book:

Amplified Bible (AMP)
Amplified Bible, Classic Edition (AMPC)
Holman Christian Standard Bible (HCSB)
King James Version (KJV)
New American Standard Bible (NASB)
New International Version (NIV)
New King James Version (NKJV)
New Revised Stand Version (NRSV)
World English Bible (WEB)
Young's Literal Translation (YLT)

Table of Contents

The Book of Revelation Devotional

The Goals of this Devotional

First, this book aims to inspire you with some of the amazing depths of meaning within the book of Revelation.

Second, the devotion seeks to challenge you with provocative questions you may not have thought to ask.

Third, the Revelation Devotional invites you to continue to explore the book with God through prayer. Even going through the book in a year will not uncover all its meaning.

How to Use this Book

You will go through the book of Revelation verse-by-verse, reviewing one or two verses per day. It's a densely packed book, and you will take time to think about each verse.

It's hard to slow down and think through each verse. Begin by reading the verse for the day twice. Does anything strike you as especially interesting or unusual? Do you have any questions? If so, write down your thoughts and impressions.

Pray for help from God. Wait for His answers. I have used the public domain World English Bible. I will occasionally add the King James Version to supply additional meaning. You can use other translations, if you wish, to help clarify any verse. I have put in my personal prayers about each verse. You can pray them yourself or use them to spark your own prayers.

To give you ideas, I pose questions on each verse that may be answered within the verse or, in Revelation, or elsewhere in the Bible. I also give you questions to which no one knows the answer. These debatable matters are not for arguing but for thinking, meditating, and praying.

Finally, I share my thoughts on each verse that came to me as I wrote this book.

Please use the blank space at the end of each page for your insights.

I welcome your feedback!

After the 366-day devotional, I have an appendix with a Scripture survey of the Book of Life .

You may use this devotional as I have arranged each page. I copied Timothy Keller's format I found in his book, *Songs of Jesus*.[5] I added the questions I'd ask of my small group. Questions are the best way to engage with Scripture. The questions may be easy and answered from within the daily verse, previous verses in Revelation, or elsewhere in the Bible. The questions may be hard, requiring you to research the Bible, use a Bible dictionary, or read a history of the first century Judea. The answers may be debatable, uncertain, or unknown. What matters is to engage your mind to think and meditate on the verse, rather than just answer the questions. Read the Scripture, think about the questions, pray, and consider my observations.

Or you can use the AAA method I learned from Timothy Keller. First, read the Scripture. Next, Adore and praise God for it. Admit any fault you perceive in yourself, Finally, Aspire to grow as a result of the Scripture.

"For the Lord himself will descend from heaven with a shout, with the voice of the archangel and with God's trumpet. The dead in Christ will rise first, then we who are alive, who are left, will be caught up together with them in the clouds, to meet the Lord in the air. So we will be with the Lord forever. Therefore comfort one another with these words." **1 Thessalonians 4:16-18**

January 1 – Revelation 1:1-2

This is the Revelation of Jesus Christ, which God gave him to show to his servants the things which must happen soon, which he sent and made known by his angel to his servant, John,[2] who testified to God's word and of the testimony of Jesus Christ, about everything that he saw.

What is the origin of the book of Revelation?

How did John get the book of Revelation? Through which Persons did the Revelation pass?

What is the purpose of the Revelation?

Who is the intended audience of Revelation?

What is in the Book of Revelation?

Prayer: Thank You, Almighty God, for giving us the book of Revelation, directly from You through Jesus Christ our Lord. Thank You for using Your created angels and sons of men to spread Your truth through all the world. Amen.

This is the Revelation of Jesus Christ: God gives us the name of the book: the Revelation of Jesus Christ. He gives us the topic, things which must happen soon, and shows the provenance of the book as the knowledge flows from His throne through Jesus, to His angel, to John, and then to the whole church.

January 2 – Revelation 1:3-4

Blessed is he who reads and those who hear the words of the prophecy, and keep the things that are written in it, for the time is at hand.[4] John, to the seven assemblies that are in Asia.

Who is blessed by this book?

1.

2.

3.

Why are these groups blessed?

What time is at hand?

To whom is John writing this book?

Prayer: Thank You, Holy Father, for blessing us for reading Your book, for blessing everyone who hears of the book, and for encouraging us to keep the things written within it. We're delighted to hear of our brethren, the seven churches of Asia Minor, preserving this book and passing it on to us today. Amen.

Blessed is he who reads and those who hear the words of the Prophecy. We need encouragement, especially in difficult times. God gives us His blessing for reading or hearing the book of Revelation, and more, for keeping what He says. This means not only obeying the commands written within it but also keeping the words and promises within our minds for meditation and hope.

January 3 – Revelation 1:4-5

Grace to you and peace from God, who is and who was and who is to come; and from the seven Spirits who are before his throne;[5] and from Jesus Christ, the faithful witness, the firstborn of the dead, and the ruler of the kings of the earth.

How does John salute the seven churches?

In Whose Names does John salute the seven churches?

1.

2.

3.

4.

5.

6.

7.

Prayer: We praise You, Holy Father, Faithful Jesus Christ, and the sevenfold Holy Spirit given to Christians and with us to the end. You have given us Your grace, Your gifts, eternal life, and all that we need in this life. You give us Your peace in the violence, war, and chaos that is in this world. We know that Jesus Christ is Ruler over all the rulers of the Earth, and we have hope in You, now and forever. Amen.

Grace to you and peace from God. Grace, *charis* in Greek, means unmerited love. These are gifts to us from the Father, Son, and Holy Spirit, along with peace from the eternal God, Who has always existed and is outside of time. Jesus is the faithful witness of these things and the firstborn of the dead. He died in our place, so that we may be forgiven and live forever. He was the ruler of the Earth. He still is and will be forever.

January 4 – Revelation 1:5-6

To him who loves us, and washed us from our sins by his blood— ⁶ and he made us to be a Kingdom, priests to his God and Father—to him be the glory and the dominion forever and ever. Amen.

How does Jesus Christ feel about His church?

What has Jesus Christ done for His church?

1.

2.

3.

To Whom is the church presented by Jesus?

How is God praised by John?

Prayer: Thank You, Lord Jesus Christ, for making us into a kingdom of priests and kings for Your Father and our Father in heaven. All glory and dominion is Yours forever and ever. Amen.

To him who loves us. The focus is on Jesus, the Author of the book of Revelation, in this verse and throughout the book. We must keep that perspective as we read through the book. Every verse is what Jesus wants us to know.

January 5 – Revelation 1:7

Behold, he is coming with the clouds, and every eye will see him, including those who pierced him. All the tribes of the earth will mourn over him. Even so, Amen.

How will Jesus return?

Who on Earth will see Him?

Who are those who pierced Him?

What will the tribes (ethnos, ethnic groups) of the Earth do when He returns? Why?

Prayer: Just as You said, our Lord Jesus Christ, You will return with clouds. You will ensure that every person on Earth sees You, including all of us responsible for Your piercing. Every nation and race will mourn over Your death for our sake. Your will be done. Amen.

Behold, he is coming with the clouds. Jesus's second coming is described. As He returns, every living person will see Him in the clouds. That event fulfills many prophecies. Seeing Jesus will also convict many people of their sins, leading to mourning and repentance. This great repentance transcends all races and nations. Through Jesus, the world finally becomes united.

January 6 - Revelation 1:8

"I am the Alpha and the Omega," says the Lord God, "who is and who was and who is to come, the Almighty."

Who is speaking?

What are His Names mentioned here?

1.

2.

3.

4.

Why is He speaking?

Prayer: O Great God Almighty, ever living One Who is the first and the last, we are in awe of You just by reading Your words. How much more will we tremble when we see You face to face? Even so, come quickly. Amen.

Says the Lord God. Jesus speaks directly to us here. If you have a red-letter Bible, which indicates Jesus's spoken words, this is a direct quote in red. Since the book is written to His Church, Jesus begins the book by reminding us Who He is.

January 7 – Revelation 1:9

I John, your brother and partner with you in the oppression, Kingdom, and perseverance in Christ Jesus, was on the isle that is called Patmos because of God's Word and the testimony of Jesus Christ.

How does John identify himself to the church?

Why does he identify this way?

Where was John?

Why was he there?

1.

2.

Prayer: How gentle You are, Holy Father! You work through human beings like Moses and John to other human beings. You know our frame and how we cannot bear Your direct Presence. How wise and how great You are to accomplish Your infinite purpose through fallible people like us! Amen.

I John, your brother and partner with you in the oppression. John tells us how he received the book. John doesn't claim his apostleship, nor his role as an elder and pastor of Ephesus, but simply as a fellow Christian suffering in exile for the sake of Jesus. He was imprisoned on Patmos because he was a leading pastor and the last living apostle in the 90s of the first century and because he testified of Jesus Christ. Christians today still suffer imprisonment for the same reasons.

January 8 – Revelation 1:10-11

I was in the Spirit on the Lord's day, and I heard behind me a loud voice, like a trumpet[11] saying, "What you see, write in a book and send to the seven assemblies: to Ephesus, Smyrna, Pergamum, Thyatira, Sardis, Philadelphia, and to Laodicea."

What did John hear?

What did the voice sound like?

What did the voice say?

Who was speaking?

Which churches were mentioned?

1.

2.

3.

4.

5.

6.

7.

Prayer: O Father, thank You for giving us Jesus Christ as the Leader of the church, Who loves us and knows us all individually. Thank You, Lord Jesus, for Your encouragement and correction, all to our benefit. In Your Holy Name, we pray. Amen.

I heard behind me a loud voice, like a trumpet. John's revelation begins with a voice like a trumpet. John is commanded to write what he sees and tell all the churches within his region of Asia Minor, which is now Turkey.

January 9 – Revelation 1:12-13

I turned to see the voice that spoke with me. Having turned, I saw seven golden lamp stands.[13] And among the lamp stands was one like a son of man, clothed with a robe reaching down to his feet, and with a golden sash around his chest.

What did John see?

Who did John see?

What did He look like?

How was He dressed?

1.

2.

Prayer: Almighty Jesus Christ, what a privilege John received: to see You face to face. Yet we all shall receive this blessing, too. Help us to grow until that day. We pray in Your Name. Amen.

Seven golden lamp stands. These are the first things John sees. Afterward, he sees the Son of man, Jesus Himself, while He lived among the apostles. Later we learn the lampstands represent the seven churches of Asia. This teaches us that if we wish to see Jesus, we need to look within His church.

January 10 – Revelation 1:14-15

His head and his hair were white as white wool, like snow. His eyes were like a flame of fire.[15] His feet were like burnished brass, as if it had been refined in a furnace. His voice was like the voice of many waters.

What did He look like?

1.

2.

3.

What did He sound like?

How would you react if you saw Him?

Prayer: Holy Father, help us love and honor and fear Jesus Christ in equal measures. Let us not hold back in neither passion, respect, nor awe before the Creator, Maker, and Savior of all mankind. In His holy name, we pray. Amen.

His eyes were like a flame of fire. Jesus does not look like His pictures. He is more awesome, powerful, and frightening than we can imagine. We as finite creatures cannot conceive of an infinite God. He is both more loving and more fearful than anything we know. We grasp Who He is in only analogies and our imagination. A face-to-face encounter is beyond what we can fathom.

January 11 – Revelation 1:16

He had seven stars in his right hand. Out of his mouth proceeded a sharp two-edged sword. His face was like the sun shining at its brightest.

What are three more details about Jesus's appearance?

1.

2.

3.

What would it be like to see the sun in its strength?

Prayer: O my Lord Jesus Christ, we cannot imagine seeing You in Your glory. Yet You are all that we need or want, and we pray You come soon. Amen.

His face was like the sun shining at its brightest. On Earth, the sun's brightness blinds us. But in outer space, the sun's full strength would soon kill us. Combined with this awesome image, we see Jesus holding seven stars in his right hand. The right hand symbolizes God's power and strength. A sharp two-edged sword comes from Jesus's mouth. What do these things mean? He soon explains them.

January 12 – Revelation 1:17

And when I saw him, I fell at his feet as dead. And he laid his right hand upon me, saying unto me, Fear not; I am the first and the last.

How did John react to the vision of Jesus?

How would you react?

What did Jesus do?

What did Jesus say?

Prayer: Almighty God, we rejoice that Your right hand of power is upon us, so that we may bear Your Presence and not fear. Amazingly, You desire our presence with You. In awe, we praise You in Jesus's Name. Amen.

And when I saw him, I fell at his feet as dead. Christ's appearance makes John fall at His feet as dead. This is Jesus's beloved disciple who cannot endure His Presence. But then Jesus strengthens and encourages him. Jesus is the Source of eternal life and we do not need to fear. His Name is the first and the last, transcending all time.

January 13 – Revelation 1:18

and the Living one. I was dead, and behold, I am alive forever and ever. Amen. I have the keys of Death and of Hades.

What other names does Jesus give?

1.

2.

What does Jesus have?

Why does Jesus say these things?

Prayer: O Holy Father, we rejoice that Jesus has conquered death and the grave, and we have no reason to ever fear anything with You. Help us to believe this and to live without fear today. We pray in Jesus's Name. Amen.

I … have the keys of hell and of death. Jesus is our pioneer of salvation. Jesus trailblazed the path of salvation for us. He lived as an ordinary, unprivileged human, as a Jew under occupation by the Roman Empire. He was tempted as we were, yet He lived without sin. He died from the torturous death on the cross, abused and ridiculed to the end. Yet He rose victorious from the grave to glory and honor and to a name higher than any other name. He asks us to be willing to die and to live for Him, just as He lived and died for us.

January 14 – Revelation 1:19

Write the things which thou hast seen, and the things which are, and the things which shall be hereafter.

What were Jesus's instructions to John?

1.

2.

3.

What does this say about the scope of the book of Revelation?

How would you feel about this assignment?

Prayer: O Father, help us to pay close attention to what Jesus says through His Word. Help us to notice carefully what has happened in the Bible, what applies to our lives today, and what is promised yet to come. Help us to change our lives to conform exactly to what Jesus did and does in every situation. Amen.

Write the things which thou hast seen. Jesus gives John his assignment in the book of Revelation. John is to have the role of secretary, or amanuensis, for Jesus. Unlike other prophets who received the word of God and spoke it to Israel or the church, John is to write the prophecy down for Jesus. Jesus already told John this was his role in **Revelation 1:1** .

January 15 - Revelation 1:20

The mystery of the seven stars which you saw in my right hand, and the seven golden lampstands is this: The seven stars are the angels of the seven assemblies. The seven lamp stands are seven assemblies.

What are the seven stars in Jesus's right hand?

What are the seven lampstands?

Were these symbols mysteries to you?

Prayer: Thank You, Holy Father, for revealing wonderful mysteries to us through Jesus Christ our Lord. We are glad the seven angels or messengers to the seven churches are completely in Your power and control, Lord Jesus. We rejoice that You stand in the middle of our churches in the past, the present, and the future. We love You for Your tender care and love. Amen.

The mystery of the seven stars. Stars have been used as symbols for angels in both the Old and New Testament. The word 'angel' means messenger. It may be the human messenger sent to each church with the book of Revelation, the lead elder of each church, or a supernatural angel appointed over each church. The churches are called lampstands This is similar to Jesus's teaching in the Sermon on the Mount.

Matthew 5:14-16 : *"You are the light of the world. A city that is set on a hill cannot be hidden.15 Nor do they light a lamp and put it under a basket, but on a lampstand, and it gives light to all who are in the house.16 Let your light so shine before men, that they may see your good works and glorify your Father in heaven."*

January 16 - Revelation 2:1

"To the angel of the assembly in Ephesus write: 'He who holds the seven stars in his right hand, he who walks among the seven golden lamp stands says these things.'"

How Does Jesus Identify Himself to the church at Ephesus?

1.

2.

Why does He identify Himself this way? What does it emphasize?

What does it mean to the church in Ephesus?

Prayer: Ever-living Lord, Jesus Christ, we are glad our church is surrounded by Your right hand of power and that You are walking with us. Help us to walk with You and to trust in Your infinite power today and forever. Amen.

"He who walks among the seven golden lampstands." Jesus is with His Church in Ephesus and every church in the next two chapters, as well as with every church in every country around the world. No matter how badly we're persecuted, what kind of natural disasters or humanly caused catastrophes occur around us, and to us, Jesus is there.

January 17 – Revelation 2:2-3

"I know your works, and your toil and perseverance, and that you can't tolerate evil men, and have tested those who call themselves apostles, and they are not, and found them false.[3] You have perseverance and have endured for my name's sake, and have not grown weary."

What are Jesus's words of encouragement to the church at Ephesus?

1.

2.

3.

4.

5.

6.

7.

8.

Prayer: Our King and God, You know every good thing we have ever done and every sacrifice we've ever made for You and other people. Nothing is hidden from Your eyes, and nothing goes unnoticed or unrewarded. We trust Your judgment completely. Amen.

"I know your works." Jesus is aware of every word we've ever said, every action we've ever done, and every thought and motivation we've ever had. Further, He has committed to rewarding us far beyond anything we have ever done for Him. His rewards are surprising and more than we deserve, so much so that we will say, "What have I ever done for you?"

Matthew 25:37 *"Then the righteous will answer him, saying, 'Lord, when did we see you hungry and feed you, or thirsty and give you a drink?"*

January 18 – Revelation 2:4

"But I have this against you, that you left your first love."

What are Jesus's words of correction for the Ephesian Church?

Does this apply to our church? To us?

Prayer: O dear Father, in the Name of Jesus Christ, let us never leave our first love. Yet, if we have, lead us back to You in the fullness of Your love. Your arms are always open toward us. Thank You for Your constant love around us. Amen.

"You left your first love." Jesus corrects His church. Such is His love for us that He cannot leave us as we are. As children who must be taught how to read, so He teaches us how to love as He does. Consistency is one aspect of His love for us. He wants us to be consistent in our love toward Him as well. This instruction is not grievous but beneficial, even if it comes with severe chastisement. Athletes must train through pain to reach their potential and so must Christians.

January 19 - Revelation 2:5-6

"Remember therefore from where you have fallen, and repent and do the first works; or else I am coming to you swiftly, and will move your lamp stand out of its place, unless you repent.[6] But this you have, that you hate the works of the Nicolaitans, which I also hate."

What does Jesus instruct the church to do?

1.

2.

3.

What will Jesus do if the church does not repent?

Who are the Nicolaitans?

Prayer: O holy Father, help us to listen to Jesus! Help us to remember how our love has decreased. Help us repent of our ways. Help us love as we did at first. Through Jesus Christ, we can do all these things. In His Name, we pray. Amen.

Remember therefore from where you have fallen. Jesus wants us to grow in love throughout our lives. If our love is diminishing, that is a serious problem He must correct. Jesus may even close a church of His and scatter the brethren if that is necessary to teach them to love.

January 20 - Revelation 2:7

"He who has an ear, let him hear what the Spirit says to the assemblies. To him who overcomes I will give to eat from the tree of life, which is in the Paradise of my God."

What is Jesus's promise for overcomers?

To whom does this promise apply?

Prayer: O great Father, how strong is Your will and purpose for mankind. You intended mankind to live forever in paradise with You, but we did not want to live under Your government, and we rebelled. You rescued us from sin through the blood of Your Son Jesus, Who will return and reign over us forever in paradise, just as You intended all along. In the Name of the King, we pray. Amen.

"He who has an ear." Jesus closes His message with encouragement. His correction does not stand alone. Regardless of the trials, persecutions, or troubles the Ephesians may face, He promises them eternal life in the paradise of God. This message is not limited to the Ephesians but goes to all the churches of Asia Minor and, by extension, to all the churches of the world.

January 21 – Revelation 2:8

"To the angel of the assembly in Smyrna write: "The first and the last, who was dead, and has come to life says these things."

How Does Jesus identify Himself?

1.

2.

What does this identity of Jesus mean to you?

Prayer: Ever-living God, Jesus Christ, You died for us so that we do not need to fear death, since You have already gone there and have come back. You knew You'd die when You made mankind, and yet You made us anyway because of Your love and Your knowledge of the glorious future ahead. Help us to always remember this is Who You are. Amen.

"The First and the Last." The Alpha and the Omega in **Revelation 22:13**. The A to Z in the English alphabet. Jesus encompasses eternity. But He also encompasses life and death. He became a human so He could die in our place. But because He is God He is now alive forevermore. We must keep this identity of Jesus Christ in mind as we read Revelation.

January 22 - Revelation 2:9

"I know your works, oppression, and your poverty (but you are rich), and the blasphemy of those who say they are Jews, and they are not, but are a synagogue of Satan."

How does Jesus encourage the church at Smyrna?

1.

2.

3.

How would you feel if you were suffering, persecuted, and poor and Jesus said this to you?

Which of Jesus's three statements do you find most encouraging?

Prayer: Holy Father, You and Jesus know everything that happens to us. You know every good thing that we think, say, or do. You know every moment of suffering and persecution. You know our poverty in this world's goods. But You tell us the reality is that we are rich, having everything we need in Jesus Christ. You know those who persecute us and that they follow Satan and will reap the same reward. Help us forever rest in the riches of Jesus Christ. Amen.

"I know." The idea of God's omniscience is alien to us and hard to imagine. Not only does He know every thought we have ever thought, every word, and deed, but He also knows that of all other people, including all our ancestors and every human being who has ever lived. He knows all motivations of every person and all our possible futures. He knows infinitely more than we do. How can we not trust Him in everything?

January 23 – Revelation 2:10

"Don't be afraid of the things which you are about to suffer. Behold, the devil is about to throw some of you into prison, that you may be tested; and you will have oppression for ten days. Be faithful to death, and I will give you the crown of life."

What are Jesus's words of exhortation to Smyrna?

1.

2.

3.

What do you find most heartening in Jesus's words?

Prayer: O Father, You teach us hundreds of times in the Bible not to fear, no matter what we face, but we cannot do this on our own. Be with us, Jesus, as You were with the disciples in the boat in the storm. Help us to rest with You in the storm of life, knowing You are in complete control. Amen.

"Don't be afraid." Jesus commands us, and then He lists what we most fear: suffering, prison, trials, and death. But Jesus has conquered death, and He wants us to conquer it, too. For beyond death is a crown of life which we will receive from the King of Kings Himself.

January 24 - Revelation 2:11

"He who has an ear, let him hear what the Spirit says to the assemblies. He who overcomes won't be harmed by the second death."

What is Jesus's promise for overcoming?

To how many of the seven churches does this apply?

Does this apply to you?

Prayer: O Father, first help us to hear You and Your word, to remember it, and to do it. Then help us to overcome all the obstacles we face that prevent us from hearing, remembering, and doing. Through the whole process of overcoming, help us have faith and trust in You, Who makes it all possible through Jesus Christ. Amen.

"He who has an ear." Do we have ears? Can we hear what the Spirit says through the Word of God? Do we believe? Remember that all things are possible through Jesus Christ Who gives us strength. Walk with Him, and He will part the sea before us.

January 25 - Revelation 2:12

"To the angel of the assembly in Pergamum write: 'He who has the sharp two-edged sword says these things.'"

How does Jesus identify Himself?

What does a sharp two-edged sword mean, both literally and symbolically?

How does this description fit with or contradict your image of Jesus?

Prayer: O Holy Father of love, let us always remember You are a God of judgment as well as love. You have given all judgment to Jesus Christ Who is over all the world's judges and authorities. Let us both love You and fear You, Jesus, as our Judge and King. Amen.

"The sharp sword two-edged sword." This is a standard Roman sword used by thousands of soldiers seen all over the empire every day. It can cut in either direction and is the official instrument of death used to kill Roman citizens who commit capital crimes. All these connotations would come to the churches who heard the book of Revelation. Then we need to add the image Jesus used in chapter one: the sharp two-edged sword coming out of His mouth that is the word of God. Think about these things.

January 26 - Revelation 2:13

"I know your works and where you dwell, where Satan's throne is. You hold firmly to my name and didn't deny my faith in the days of Antipas my witness, my faithful one, who was killed among you, where Satan dwells."

Do you believe Jesus knows your works and where you live?

Where did the Pergamos church live?

What other works of the Pergamos church did Jesus cite?

1.

2.

Prayer: O holy Jesus, help us remember You know everything about us, every good deed we have ever done, and all the persecutions we have suffered for the sake of Your name. Help us to be a courageous witness of You, even to our death. Help us focus on the life You have given us and not on bodily death. In Your beautiful Name, I pray. Amen.

"I know your works and where you dwell." Jesus's words of encouragement are to the church at Pergamos and us. There was a major Roman headquarter in this city and a large temple of pagan worship. Christians there were marked for not participating in temple ceremonies and were considered traitors and atheists who didn't believe in the Roman gods. Jesus knew about their faithful suffering and testimony to His name, and He recognized it for all eternity. He will acknowledge our testimony in our society, which is also of Satan.

January 27 – Revelation 2:14-15

"But I have a few things against you, because you have there some who hold the teaching of Balaam, who taught Balak to throw a stumbling block before the children of Israel, to eat things sacrificed to idols, and to commit sexual immorality.[15] So you also have some who hold to the teaching of the Nicolaitans likewise."

Are you familiar with how Balaam got Israel to sin against God? If not, review Numbers 25:1-3. Summarize his technique here:

How could this doctrine be applied to deceive Christians?

Prayer: O Father, help us to cleave to Jesus and His word and not deviate from it no matter what men may say. Keep us from being deceived. In Jesus's Name, we pray. Amen.

"The teaching of Balaam" is to get as close as possible to sin. This led Israel to sin with idolatry and fornication. So some false teachers say to Christians that sin or some sin is acceptable. Notice Jesus opposes this vehemently.

January 28 – Revelation 2:16

"Repent therefore, or else I am coming to you quickly, and I will make war against them with the sword of my mouth."

What is Jesus's single command to those who hold the doctrine of Balaam or the Nicolaitans?

What will Jesus do with those who do not repent of their sin?

What is the sword of Jesus's mouth?

Prayer: Help us repent, Father, not only of these sins but of all our sins which we commit. Purify our hearts so that we don't even want to sin anymore. Only by Your miraculous power through the Holy Spirit can we do this. In Jesus's Name, we pray. Amen.

I will make war against them with the sword of my mouth. Jesus's sword from His mouth is the Word of God.

Hebrews 4:12 *For the word of God is living and powerful, and sharper than any two-edged sword, piercing even to the division of soul and spirit, and of joints and marrow, and is a discerner of the thoughts and intents of the heart. (KJV)*

January 29 – Revelation 2:17

"He who has an ear, let him hear what the Spirit says to the assemblies. To him who overcomes, to him I will give of the hidden manna, and I will give him a white stone, and on the stone a new name written, which no one knows but he who receives it."

To which church or churches does Jesus address this overcoming message?

To what does "hidden manna" refer?

To what does the "white stone" refer?

What would it mean to you to have a special name given to you by Jesus, which only you and He know?

Prayer: O dear Father in heaven, help us to listen to the Spirit! Help us to overcome our failings and weaknesses! Lead us to that day when we may eat the hidden manna, the bread from heaven, and receive a new name from the King of Kings Himself, Jesus Christ. In His Name, we pray. Amen.

"I will give him a white stone." The local custom in the Pergamos church was to give white stones as recognition and respect. How marvellously Jesus has written this book through John so that the words apply very specifically to the local churches in Asia Minor, and at the same time to all churches through the millennia since the book was written!

January 30 - Revelation 2:18

"To the angel of the assembly in Thyatira write: 'The Son of God, who has his eyes like a flame of fire, and his feet are like burnished brass, says these things.'"

How Does Jesus identify Himself?

1.

2.

3.

How would you feel if Jesus said this to you?

What would you do?

Prayer: Dear Father, help me to listen to Jesus's every word and treat each with respect and awe. My Lord Jesus Christ, enable me to keep my eyes on You and not things of this

world. Amen .

"The Son of God." Jesus Christ was born of a woman and died as a man. He was condemned as a criminal on a cross and buried in a borrowed grave. Yet He came from God, was God, came back to life as God, and reigns as God. He retains His human memories, feelings, and nature, perfectly united with His God nature. Amazingly, we generally take Him, His words, and His deeds too lightly.

January 31 - Revelation 2:19

"I know your works, your love, faith, service, patient endurance, and that your last works are more than the first."

What are Jesus's words of encouragement for Thyatira?

1.

2.

3.

4.

5.

6.

7.

Prayer: Dear Father, nothing escapes You and Jesus Christ. You know all our good works, all our attempts at good works, and all our failures while trying to do good. You know all our good traits, and You treasure and mark each one. You also note our growth, year by year and decade by decade. You know every obstacle we face and all our persecutions. Help us to remember these things when we grow weary and discouraged in trying to do good with no acknowledgment or recognition. In Jesus's Name, we pray. Amen.

"I know Your works." Jesus says this to Thyatira and every Christian. He next mentions our charity, *charis*, in Greek, our love, our desire to give to and bless others. This is our motivation. Our service to others is one example of works and charity working together. Our faith in God is another motivation for our works. Our patience is the fruit of faith over time. We continue to believe and serve for years and decades. Jesus mentions works again and that their latter works are more than their first.

February 1 – Revelation 2:20-21

"But I have this against you, that you tolerate your woman, Jezebel, who calls herself a prophetess. She teaches and seduces my servants to commit sexual immorality, and to eat things sacrificed to idols.[21] I gave her time to repent, but she refuses to repent of her sexual immorality."

What does the false prophetess Jezebel do?

1.

2.

3.

4.

5.

Prayer: Father, protect us, defend us, from false prophets and prophetesses who teach contrary to Your word. Let us neither be deceived nor give in to convenience or lust to indulge in these sins. In Jesus's Name, the Holy One of God, we pray. Amen.

"Who calls herself a prophetess." Jesus says this of Jezebel. There were prophetesses in both the Old and New Testaments, so that office isn't bad — unless it is a lie. Since a prophet's job is to speak the words of God to people, and we know she wasn't doing this, she is lying. Anyone who teaches people to commit fornication (sex outside of marriage) and to sacrifice to idols, (goods, money, food, to anything that is worshiped other than God) is opposing God.

February 2 - Revelation 2:21-22

"I gave her time to repent, but she refuses to repent of her sexual immorality.[22] Behold, I will throw her and those who commit adultery with her into a bed of great oppression, unless they repent of her works."

What did God do with Jezebel?

What did she do in return?

What will God do next?

Why does God do this?

Prayer: O Father, lead us into repentance daily. Help us to hear the words of Jesus and to change our behavior before Jesus's judgment falls upon us. If we are in tribulation, let us use the opportunity to repent of our deeds before God. O save us, in Jesus's Name. Amen.

"I gave her space to repent of her fornication." Jesus says this of the false prophetess Jezebel. Her name reminds us of Ahab's wife, who lured Ahab and all of Israel into worshipping Baal. (See **1 Kings 17-19**.) This sin of fornication can refer to worshipping gods other than the Lord God, Jesus. Both Israel and the Church are in a marriage covenant with Jesus Christ, and to have another god ahead of Him is to commit adultery against Him.

February 3 – Revelation 2:23

"I will kill her children with Death, and all the assemblies will know that I am he who searches the minds and hearts. I will give to each one of you according to your deeds."

Who are the children of Jezebel?

Why does Jesus kill these children?

1.

2.

Prayer: O Father, let us pay attention to everyone who dies and consider our works and the fruits of our works. Are our works leading us to death? Help us to repent before it is too late, Lord Jesus. Let us be faithful to You and nothing else. Amen.

"All the assemblies shall know that I am He Who searches the minds and hearts." Sadly, it often takes death or the threat of death to seriously consider our lifestyle. Jesus holds our lives in His hand, and He wants us to repent. For His standard is death for sin, which He suffered for our sake so we could be forgiven. Do we intend to continue in sin and suffer death despite His sacrifice?

February 4 – Revelation 2:24-25

"But to you, I say, to the rest who are in Thyatira, as many as don't have this teaching, who don't know what some call "the deep things of Satan," to you I say, I am not putting any other burden on you.[25] Nevertheless, hold that which you have firmly until I come."

What are Jesus's two statements of encouragement to Thyatira?

1.

2.

What is the difference between those in Thyatira receiving encouragement and those receiving correction from Jesus?

Prayer: O Father, let us utterly reject Satan and all his works and doctrine and wholly surrender to our King, Jesus Christ. Help us to hold fast to the goodness He has given us until He comes. Amen.

"As many as don't have this teaching." There are those in Jesus's churches that have false doctrines from Satan and those that do not. Jesus draws a sharp distinction between them, urging those with false beliefs to repent and encouraging those with truth to hold on until He returns.

February 5 – Revelation 2:26-29

"He who overcomes, and he who keeps my works to the end, to him I will give authority over the nations.[27] He will rule them with a rod of iron, shattering them like clay pots; as I also have received of my Father:[28] and I will give him the morning star.[29] He who has an ear, let him hear what the Spirit says to the assemblies."

What does Jesus promise to those who overcome and keep His works to the end?

1.

2.

3.

To Whom does Jesus compare the ruling authority of the overcomers?

What is this "morning star" Jesus gives?

Prayer: O Father, we're in awe of the gifts Jesus gives to His overcomers. Help us believe this applies to each one of us, despite our very ordinary lives and small accomplishments. Help us hold on to this promise although all the world opposes Jesus. In His Name, we pray, Amen.

"He will rule them with a rod of iron." Jesus promises a rod of iron—of rulership over all nations for His overcomers. The rod is what a shepherd uses to lead and protect his sheep. It was taken as a symbol of rulership by the kings of the earth. This is exactly what the Father gives to Jesus.

Psalm 2:9 *Thou shalt break them with a rod of iron; thou shalt dash them in pieces like a potter's vessel.*

We will go from powerlessness over the evil of the world to breaking the evil forever.

February 6 - Revelation 3:1

And to the angel of the assembly in Sardis write: "He who has the seven Spirits of God and the seven stars says these things: "I know your works, that you have a reputation of being alive, but you are dead."

How does Jesus identify Himself to the church at Sardis?

1.

2.

What good things of Sardis does Jesus recognize?

1.

2.

What is Sardis's failing?

Prayer: O Father, wake us up from the dead! Help us live up to the living name of Jesus Christ and not live like people who don't know You. Let us not fear physical death, but instead being spiritually dead and unconnected with You. In the name of Jesus, we pray. Amen.

"He that has the seven Spirits of God and the seven stars." There are not seven Holy Spirits, but one Spirit with seven flames, like the menorah in the temple. The seven stars are the seven angels or messengers of the churches. Jesus is with our church through His Spirit and His angels He sends to us. How can we fall asleep in His Presence?

February 7 – Revelation 3:2

"Wake up and keep the things that remain, which you were about to throw away, for I have found no works of yours perfected before my God."

What two things does Jesus command Sardis?

1.

2.

What does Jesus say is their root problem? Why are they about to die?

Prayer: O Eternal Father, strong to save, perfect our works in Jesus Christ! Help us be watchful of our life and root out all behavior that is not like Jesus, which is not loving, which is not patient or kind. Let us not die as a church, but instead do the work you've given us from the beginning. In Jesus's Name, we pray. Amen.

"Keep the things which remain." We are to persist in doing good: helping the poor and sick and preaching the good news of the kingdom of God to those who do not know the truth. If we cease doing these things, we will be a dead church.

February 8 – Revelation 3:3

"Remember therefore how you have received and heard. Keep it and repent. If therefore you won't watch, I will come as a thief, and you won't know what hour I will come upon you."

What are the three additional commands Jesus gives to Sardis?

1.

2.

3.

Prayer: O Father, help us remember Your teaching, Your calling, how You called us to Jesus, and how we were at the beginning of our Christian lives. Let us hold to our original zeal and behavior and never let it go. Let us see where we've departed from Your teaching and turn back to You. Help us repent, holy Father, in Jesus's Name! Amen.

"If you shall not watch I will come on you as a thief, and you shall not know what hour I come upon you." If we don't do the work Jesus gives us, if we don't watch for opportunities to serve others and preach the gospel, we lose sight of Jesus. He will visit us suddenly and call us to account.

February 9 - Revelation 3:4

"Nevertheless you have a few names in Sardis that didn't defile their garments. They will walk with me in white, for they are worthy."

What is the reward for those in Sardis who are worthy?

What does it mean to walk with Jesus in white?

What does it mean to defile one's garments as a Christian? (Hint: Revelation 19:8)

Prayer: Father in heaven, help us to live out the righteousness of Jesus, which You have given to us. Let our behavior be like His, let our words be His, and let our attitude be His. Then the world may see Jesus in us. In His holy Name, we pray. Amen.

"A few names in Sardis" Although Jesus calls Sardis a dead church, some are alive in Him. So a church may have fallen asleep in doing the work of God, yet a few individuals remain, whom God notices. Thus, if we feel we are the only ones following Jesus in our church, that is okay; God notices.

February 10 – Revelation 3:5-6

"He who overcomes will be arrayed in white garments, and I will in no way blot his name out of the book of life, and I will confess his name before my Father, and before his angels.[6] He who has an ear, let him hear what the Spirit says to the assemblies."

What does Jesus promise to the overcomer?

1.

2.

3.

To whom are Jesus and the Holy Spirit speaking?

Prayer: O Lord Jesus, help us to hold on to Your promises to overcome so that even when we're exhausted and can't do anything, we can stand in You. Give us the power we need, and encourage our hearts with the vision of standing before You in white clothing, hearing You praise our name to the Father. In Jesus's Name, we pray. Amen.

"He that overcomes shall be clothed with white clothing." This verse was cited yesterday:

Revelation 19:8 And to her it was granted to be arrayed in fine linen, clean and bright, for the fine linen is the righteous acts of the saints.

Jesus will clothe us according to our righteous acts. If it seems impossible for us to be righteous, remember all our sins are forgiven when we believe in Jesus as our Savior, and He imputes His righteousness to us. As we obey Him, we do righteous deeds, which He planned for us to do.

February 11 – Revelation 3:7

"To the angel of the assembly in Philadelphia write: 'He who is holy, he who is true, he who has the key of David, he who opens and no one can shut, and who shuts and no one opens, says these things.'"

How does Jesus identify Himself?

1.

2.

3.

4.

5.

Prayer: O holy and true Father, Your Son is holy and true, for He faithfully follows You. Help us to be the same and faithfully follow Him through whatever open door He gives us to pass through.

"The Key of David." This is a quote from **Isaiah** 22:20-23: *That I will call My servant Eliakim the son of Hilkiah;²¹ I will clothe him with your robe And strengthen him with your belt; I will commit your responsibility into his hand. He shall be a father to the inhabitants of Jerusalem and to the house of Judah.²² The key of the house of David I will lay on his shoulder; So he shall open, and no one shall shut; And he shall shut, and no one shall open.²³ I will fasten him as a peg in a secure place, And he will become a glorious throne to his father's house.*

Jesus identifies Himself as the fulfillment of this ancient prophecy, the true heir of David and ruler of Jerusalem and Judah.

February 12 – Revelation 3:8

"I know your works (behold, I have set before you an open door, which no one can shut), that you have a little power, and kept my word, and didn't deny my name."

What does Jesus tell the church in Philadelphia?

1.

2.

3.

4.

5.

6.

How would this make you feel if Jesus said this to you?

Prayer: O Lord, our God, thank You for watching us and noting every little thing we do. Thank You for opening a door before us. Help us to walk through it today with our little strength. We will never deny the name of Jesus Who has saved us. Amen.

"I have set before you an open door." Jesus Himself opens the door for us. He doesn't make us get up and walk through them. If we see an opportunity to help someone, to show the love of God, or to encourage someone, even if we're not the best person for the job, we should take it.

February 13 – Revelation 3:9

"Behold, I give some of the synagogue of Satan, of those who say they are Jews, and they are not, but lie—behold, I will make them to come and worship before your feet, and to know that I have loved you."

What will God do to this lying synagogue (congregation) of Satan?

1.

2.

What will be the effect of these actions upon these liars?

When will this happen?

Prayer: O Father, let us hold on to Your Truth, Your Son Jesus Christ. Let us not be deceived by Satan's society and lies. You, Yourself, Lord Jesus, will correct the liars and show them their errors, in Your time. Amen.

"Which say they are Jews, and are not." Few things are more common than people who claim to be Christians and are not. Christians are Jews, for we are in Christ and grafted into the olive tree of Israel. Jews have the oracles and promises of God. Some people are sincere in their false beliefs, but many know they are putting on an act, a lie. When they are confronted by Jesus with their lie, they will be humbled and repent and come to true Christianity.

February 14 – Revelation 3:10

"Because you kept my command to endure, I also will keep you from the hour of testing which is to come on the whole world, to test those who dwell on the earth."

What does Jesus promise Philadelphia?

What is this hour of testing upon all the world?

Why does Jesus give them this promise?

Prayer: O Holy Father, help us keep Jesus's word faithfully to the end of our lives. Regardless of whether this hour of temptation for the world comes in our lifetimes, help us to be faithful to Him. In Jesus's Name, we pray. Amen.

"The hour of temptation which shall come upon all the world." Jesus Himself reveals the meaning of this phrase in His Olivet prophecy:

Matthew 24:21-22 For then there will be great tribulation, such as has not been since the beginning of the world until this time, no, nor ever shall be.22 And unless those days were shortened, no flesh would be saved; but for the elect's sake, those days will be shortened.

The "elect" are Christians. That means they are selected or chosen by God, just like Abraham, Isaac, and Jacob.

February 15 – Revelation 3:11

"I am coming quickly! Hold firmly that which you have, so that no one takes your crown."

What does Jesus promise?

What does Jesus command?

What is the consequence of not obeying Jesus's command?

Prayer: O holy Father, let us always be ready for Jesus's return, waiting in expectation and holding on to the calling You've given us. Let us never deny Your Name but let us walk through the doors that Jesus opens. In the Name of our King, we pray. Amen.

"Hold firmly that which you have." What does the Philadelphia church have? From verses 8-10 we read: 1) thy works, 2) for thou hast a little strength, 3) and hast kept my word, 4) and hast not denied my name. 5) Thou hast kept the word of my patience. We must examine ourselves. Do we have these things? Are they growing or are we losing them?

February 16 – Revelation 3:12-13

"He who overcomes, I will make him a pillar in the temple of my God, and he will go out from there no more. I will write on him the name of my God and the name of the city of my God, the new Jerusalem, which comes down out of heaven from my God, and my own new name.[13] He who has an ear, let him hear what the Spirit says to the assemblies."

What does a pillar do in a building?

What does it mean to have God's name written on us?

What does it mean to have the new Jerusalem's name written on us?

What does it mean to have Jesus's new name written on us?

What does it mean that Jesus does this personally to each overcomer?

Prayer: Father in heaven, help us to be overcomers that please our Lord and King Jesus Christ from now until His return. Let us never depart from Your temple, Your church, of which Jesus is the Chief Cornerstone. In His Name, we pray. Amen.

"A pillar in the temple." There were two decorative pillars at the entrance of the Temple with the names meaning "he will establish" and "strength."[4] Applying these names to Christian overcomers—who begin as the weak of the world, wholly dependent upon God throughout their lives—is appropriate. The overcomers become pillars through God establishing His strength in them.

February 17 – Revelation 3:14

To the angel of the assembly in Laodicea write: "The Amen, the Faithful and True Witness, the Beginning[1] of God's creation, says these things."

How does Jesus identify Himself?

1.

2.

3.

Prayer: O Father, help us to listen to Jesus, to fully hear Him, and to follow and obey Him. He is the Truth, having made all that is. We pray in the Name of our Ruler, Jesus Christ. Amen.

"The Source of God's creation." Just as Eden had four rivers coming from a single source, so all the universe comes from a single origin: Jesus Christ. We often read Jesus's words and commands without realizing He is the ultimate authority about humanity and how we must live.

---

[1] Source or Head, WEB footnote.

February 18 – Revelation 3:15

"I know your works, that you are neither cold nor hot. I wish you were cold or hot."

What does "cold" mean in the context of the works of a church?

What does "hot" mean in the context of the works of a church?

Why is "warm" worse for church works than cold or hot?

Prayer: O holy Father, help us to be boiling with fervency for Your work and not lukewarm, only dabbling in the good works You love. Let our whole hearts be devoted to You and not divided between You and anything else in the world. In Jesus's Name, we pray. Amen.

"I wish you were cold or hot." What seems to be a metaphorical description of church works has a very literal application in the ancient city of Laodicea. From Wikipedia:

"This metaphor has been drawn from the water supply of the city, which was lukewarm, in contrast to the hot springs at nearby Hierapolis and the cold, pure waters of Colossae.[8] The archaeology shows that Laodicea had an aqueduct that probably carried water from hot mineral springs some five miles south, which would have become tepid before entering the city (See main Laodicea article.).[9] The imagery of the Laodicean aqueduct suggests not that "hot" is good and "cold" is bad, but that both hot and cold water are useful."[15]

Thus, both the cold spring water and the hot spring water were lukewarm by the time they got to Laodicea. The cold water would be refreshing, and the hot water was good medicinally. Warm water was useless. Are we ever useless to Christ?

February 19 – Revelation 3:16-17

"So, because you are lukewarm, and neither hot nor cold, I will vomit you out of my mouth.[17] Because you say, 'I am rich, and have gotten riches, and have need of nothing'; and don't know that you are the wretched one, miserable, poor, blind, and naked.'"

What will Jesus do with the Laodiceans?

What do the Laodiceans think about themselves?

1.

2.

3.

What does Jesus think of the Laodiceans?

1.

2.

3.

Prayer: Father in heaven, help us to listen to Jesus and not be comfortable where we are. Help us to see ourselves as You see us and take action and repent. In the Name of my Savior, we pray. Amen.

"I will vomit you out of my mouth." The Greek word is *emeo* from which we get our word emetic. It means vomit. Why does Jesus use such an image? First, the lukewarm water Laodicea got from Hierapolis' hot springs still had many dissolved minerals in it, which caused vomiting in those not used to it. The church knew this reaction on visitors to the city. Second, Jesus says their self-image is self-satisfied when in reality they are revolting. Jesus cannot partake of deceit but vomits it out. Are we self-deceived?

February 20 – Revelation 3:18

"I counsel you to buy from me gold refined by fire, that you may become rich; and white garments, that you may clothe yourself, and that the shame of your nakedness may not be revealed; and eye salve to anoint your eyes, that you may see."

What is gold tried in fire from Jesus?

What are white garments from Jesus?

What is the eye salve from Jesus?

Prayer: O Father, help us give our all to Jesus—our whole lives, holding nothing back. Jesus held nothing back from us and will give us all we need. In the Name of our King, we pray. Amen.

"I counsel thee to buy of me gold tried in the fire." Gold symbolizes our faith as Peter says:

1 Peter 1:7 *that the proof of your faith, which is more precious than gold that perishes even though it is tested by fire, may be found to result in praise, glory, and honor at the revelation of Jesus Christ.*

Likewise, white garments are explained:

Revelation 19:8 *And to her was granted that she should be arrayed in fine linen, clean and white: for the fine linen is the righteousness of saints.*

And what of the eye salve that Jesus offers?

John 9:5-7 *As long as I am in the world, I am the light of the world."⁶ When He had said these things, He spat on the ground and made clay with the saliva; and He anointed the eyes of the blind man with the clay.⁷ And He said to him, "Go, wash in the pool of Siloam" (which is translated, Sent). So he went and washed, and came back seeing.*

John 9:39 *And Jesus said, "For judgment I have come into this world, that those who do not see may see, and that those who see may be made blind."*

February 21 – Revelation 3:19

"As many as I love, I reprove and chasten. Be zealous therefore, and repent."

Whom does Jesus love?

Whom does Jesus rebuke and chasten?

How should we respond to Jesus's rebuke?

Prayer: Father, help us so that we are not discouraged when we are chastened for our sins, but help us rejoice that Jesus loves us enough to correct us from our sins and lead us to righteousness.

"As many as I love, I rebuke and chasten." This is not how we usually think of Jesus loving us: correcting us for our sins. Those who study the letters to the churches usually think of Laodicea as the "bad church." But Jesus specifically tells them He loves them. His love encourages us to repent.

February 22 – Revelation 3:20

"Behold, I stand at the door and knock. If anyone hears my voice and opens the door, then I will come in to him, and will dine with him, and he with me."

Which door is Jesus standing in front of and knocking?

Who can open this door to Jesus?

What will Jesus do in response to this open door?

Prayer: Infinite Creator, Ruler of the universe, help us to hear Jesus knocking on our doors. Let us not delay, but immediately open our doors to Him and allow Him in our minds, our hearts, and our lives, forever. In Jesus's Name, the God who knocks, we pray. Amen.

"I will come in to him, and will sup with him, and he with me." With whom do we eat? Is it not our closest family members and best friends? Are we ready to have Jesus as our best friend, as our closest family member and companion? Why wouldn't we want this?

February 23 – Revelation 3:21-22

"He who overcomes, I will give to him to sit down with me on my throne, as I also overcame, and sat down with my Father on his throne.[22] He who has an ear, let him hear what the Spirit says to the assemblies."

What does Jesus promise to anyone who overcomes?

What does the Father rule from His throne?

What does Jesus rule from His throne?

Who is commanded to listen to this message?

Prayer: Holy Father in heaven, not only do you rule the universe from Your throne but also all that You will create through all eternity. Further, You have promised Jesus's kingdom will continually increase, so we can expect new things for all eternity. We worship You in awe, infinite God! In Jesus's Name, we pray. Amen.

"He that has an ear, let him hear what the Spirit says." Jesus's command to listen is not limited to the churches listed in Revelation but extends to all mankind. Who doesn't want infinite, ruling, creating power for all eternity, filled with new challenges? God loves all humanity and gives His promises to all of us.

February 24 – Revelation 4:1

After these things I looked and saw a door opened in heaven, and the first voice that I heard, like a trumpet speaking with me, was one saying, "Come up here, and I will show you the things which must happen after this."

"After this" refers to what?

Where was this open door?

Where was John?

Who was talking to John?

What will John see next?

Prayer: Our Father, open the book of Revelation to us so we may understand all that John saw. We pray for understanding to testify about Jesus and so perform Your work, our work, on earth. In Jesus's Name, the Revelator, we pray. Amen.

"Things which must happen after this." Jesus shows us the future, beginning at the time John was on Patmos. Remember Jesus gave this message for His church through John. Therefore the church needs this message and knowledge. Just as the letters apply to all the churches and all mankind, so this message goes to the church and all mankind.

February 25 - Revelation 4:2

Immediately I was in the Spirit. Behold, there was a throne set in heaven, and one sitting on the throne.

What does "in the Spirit" mean?

What did John see?

1.

2.

Where was John?

How does this vision connect to Revelation 3:21?

Prayer: Father, we often pray or say that "God is on His throne," but here Scripture reveals You ruling Your creation. You are never idle but work every day, as does Jesus Christ. Help us to be about our work, whatever You've given us to do. In Jesus's Name, we ask this. Amen.

Behold, a throne was set in heaven. There are no thrones in the atmosphere, nor outer space, so this vision must be of the third heaven, where God rules. We must be careful to orient our thoughts to each shift of location in Revelation to properly understand what is happening in each vision. Like other prophetic visions, the point of view shifts frequently and abruptly, as it does here.

February 26 - Revelation 4:3

That looked like a jasper stone and a sardius. There was a rainbow around the throne, like an emerald to look at.

How does God appear upon His throne?

How does His throne appear?

Why is there a rainbow around the throne?

Prayer: O Most High Father, let us remember Your awesome beauty as we pray to You each day. Even in the middle of ruling the universe, You arrange glorious colors all around You. You do everything perfectly. Amen

There was a rainbow around the throne. Like many symbols in the book of Revelation, the rainbow is explained elsewhere in the Bible, way back in Genesis:

Genesis 9:12-16 *God said, "This is the token of the covenant which I make between me and you and every living creature that is with you, for perpetual generations:*[13] *I set my rainbow in the cloud, and it will be a sign of a covenant between me and the earth.*[14] *When I bring a cloud over the earth, that the rainbow will be seen in the cloud,*[15] *I will remember my covenant, which is between me and you and every living creature of all flesh, and the waters will no more become a flood to destroy all flesh.*[16] *The rainbow will be in the cloud. I will look at it, that I may remember the everlasting covenant between God and every living creature of all flesh that is on the earth."*

So God has a rainbow around His throne to remind him of His covenant with Noah and mankind.

February 27 – Revelation 4:4

Around the throne were twenty-four thrones. On the thrones were twenty-four elders sitting, dressed in white garments, with crowns of gold on their heads.

How many elders were seated next to God's throne?

How were they clothed?

What did they have on their heads?

What do their attire and location signify?

Prayer: O Holy Father, thank You for allowing us to come close to Your throne through Jesus Christ our Savior. We don't yet have our reward or position that Jesus promised, but help us to be faithful to You and Your work until that day. In Jesus's Name, we pray. Amen.

On the thrones were twenty-four elders sitting. The twenty-four elders mirror the twenty-four courses of the priests David set up in **1 Chronicles 24:1-19**. Since the temple and the tabernacle were to picture God's throne in heaven, here we see the reality behind the twenty-four courses of priests. Just as priests serve in the temple, in the Holy Place, and the holy of holies, so these priests serve God in heaven.

February 28 - Revelation 4:5

Out of the throne proceed lightnings, sounds, and thunders. There were seven lamps of fire burning before his throne, which are the seven Spirits of God

What is your first impression of this vision of God's throne?

Where else in the Bible are there seven lamps in the presence of God's throne ?

1.

2.

Prayer: O Father, every time we come before You in prayer, we come through Your seven-fold Spirit to Your all-powerful throne. Help us to come boldly and yet with awe and humility, knowing Jesus opened the way for us, because of Your great love for us. In the Name of Jesus Christ, we pray. Amen.

Out of the throne proceed lightnings, sounds, and thunders. Why would God's throne be this way? One practical reason is the law God has made for the universe: energy flows from a greater source to a region of lesser energy. God is the source of all energy, an infinite amount. Naturally, energy will flow from Him outward. This is also a display of His power which glorifies Him before all heaven.

February 29 – Revelation 4:6

Before the throne was something like a sea of glass, similar to crystal. In the middle of the throne, and around the throne were four living creatures full of eyes before and behind.

Why would God make living creatures full of eyes?

Where else in the Bible are four creatures with many eyes mentioned ?

1.

2.

Prayer: O Holy Creator, Your power is so great, Your attendants around You are full of power and might. They must be, to serve so closely to You and to endure Your blazing energy. Further, You bless them with a unique perception of many eyes, which You fill up with Your glory. Fill up our eyes with Your glory, as well, in Jesus's Name, we pray. Amen.

Before the throne was something like a sea of glass, similar to crystal. Every king or judge in the ancient world had a court where decisions and judgments were made. Today, the president has his cabinet of advisors, and the prime minister has his or her privy council. Here we see God's government on display, with His attendants: the twenty-four elders and four creatures by the throne. The sea of glass provides room for those who come and go before Him.

March 1 – Revelation 4:7

The first creature was like a lion, and the second creature like a calf, and the third creature had a face like a man, and the fourth was like a flying eagle.

Have you ever heard of creatures that looked like these in the Bible or outside?

Are any of these creatures pictured in the Temple or the Tabernacle?

Are any of these creatures shown in Eden? (Genesis 2-3)

Prayer: Father, thank You for giving us mysteries in the book of Revelation, in the Bible, and in the world. Through these puzzles, our minds will work and grow as we search out the why and how and what and when of Your creation. Amen.

The first creature was like a lion. A flying lion occurs in Daniel's prophecy in **Daniel 7**. Another occurs in Ezekiel's visions in **Ezekiel 1:4-11**. Ezekiel in **Ezekiel 10:1** identifies these creatures as cherubim. This means they were in Eden in **Genesis 3:24** and in the tabernacle and temple over the mercy seat above the Ark of God. Note these cherubim have four wings. That information will be important to remember with tomorrow's verse.

March 2 – Revelation 4:8

The four living creatures, each one of them having six wings, are full of eyes around and within. They have no rest day and night, saying, "Holy, holy, holy is the Lord God, the Almighty, who was and who is and who is to come!"

How many wings do cherubim have?

How many wings do these creatures have?

Is there anywhere else in the Bible where there are creatures with six wings?

Prayer: How wonderful You are, God, in that You make creatures who can come into Your Presence and survive. How wonderful it is that they desire to praise You day and night. So let us praise You while we have breath: Holy, holy, holy, Lord God, the Almighty, Who was and Who is and Who is to come! Amen.

Each one of them having six wings. There is one other place in the Bible that describes and names these creatures:

Isaiah 6:1-4 I saw the Lord sitting on a throne, high and lifted up; and his train filled the temple.² Above him stood the seraphim. Each one had six wings. With two he covered his face. With two he covered his feet. With two he flew.³ One called to another, and said, "Holy, holy, holy, is Yahweh of Armies! The whole earth is full of his glory!"⁴ The foundations of the thresholds shook at the voice of him who called, and the house was filled with smoke.

These creatures are called seraphim. Notice that one is so powerful his voice shakes the foundation of the temple, which are huge stones on top of bedrock.

March 3 – Revelation 4:9-10

When the living creatures give glory, honor, and thanks to him who sits on the throne, to him who lives forever and ever,[10] the twenty-four elders fall down before him who sits on the throne, and worship him who lives forever and ever, and throw their crowns before the throne.

What happens when the four creatures give praise to God?

Who worships God?

How do they worship God?

Prayer: O Father in heaven, let us also worship You day by day and throughout the day, falling before You and giving our whole lives to You again and again. In Jesus's Name, we pray. Amen.

The four and twenty elders fall down before Him that sat on the throne. And so do we, each time we worship God. Our posture may be kneeling, prostrate, standing, or sitting, but our hearts are wholly surrendered. We cast our crowns, our lives, and our accomplishments before God, as we give him everything we are. Our Father deserves no less.

March 4 – Revelation 4:10-11

[10] Saying,[11] "Worthy are you, our Lord and God, the Holy One, to receive the glory, the honor, and the power, for you created all things, and because of your desire they existed, and were created!"

What has God created?

Why has God created the universe?

What does that mean to us?

Prayer: O Holy Lord and Father of all creation, there is nothing You haven't created. All that You created is for Your pleasure, and we exist for You — but we sin, which mars us and gives You grief. Help us remember when we're tempted by sin that we do not exist for ourselves, but for Your sake and Your pleasure. Help us to live for Your sake, not our own, for there we will find our greatest joy. In Jesus's Name, we pray. Amen.

"Worthy are you, our Lord and God, the Holy One, to receive the glory, the honor, and the power." From whom is God worthy to receive glory, honor, and power? The twenty-four elders say this, and this applies to all of God's creation, especially His sentient creatures, angels, and humanity. We have no existence without Him — from the beginning, throughout our lives, and into the eternal future. Every pleasure, every joy, we experience comes from Him.

March 5 - Revelation 5:1

And I saw in the right hand of him that sat on the throne a book written within and on the backside, sealed with seven seals.

Who creates this book with seven seals?

Who seals this book with seven seals?

Who holds this book with seven seals?

Prayer: We marvel that John was permitted to see You in heaven, Holy Father! Yet we all shall see You as You are, for John wrote we shall see You in His letter, and seeing us face to face is Your desire. Your love for us is the most amazing thing about You! We praise You with all our hearts! Amen.

I saw in the right hand of him that sat on the throne a book written. This is God our Father, the one to Whom we pray. His right hand represents His infinite power. In it, He holds this book, sealed with seven seals. We will soon discover what it contains. Introducing this mystery at this point grabs our attention. The fullness of the contents of this book is not given until the end of Chapter 16.

March 6 – Revelation 5:2

I saw a mighty angel proclaiming with a loud voice, "Who is worthy to open the book, and to break its seals?"

Who is worthy to take the book from God our Father?

Who is worthy and able to break the seven seals, created by God Himself?

What does the book contain?

Prayer: O Father Most High, it is to Your glory that You create mysteries for the citizens of heaven and Earth. You guide those who seek to know these things to a fuller understanding, but in Your wisdom, You hide them from those who do not seek You. We praise You in the Name of Jesus Christ! Amen.

Who is worthy? A Personage who is worthy must be able to go into God's Presence and must have the power of God to open seals that God Himself set. This Person is uniquely chosen by God for this purpose. Who can it be?

March 7 – Revelation 5:3

No one in heaven above, or on the earth, or under the earth, was able to open the book or to look in it.

Who isn't worthy or able to open the book?

Why aren't angels worthy?

Why aren't men worthy to open the book?

Prayer: Father, You reach out to men, but men reject You. You are holy, but we are sinful, separated from You by our sin. How great You are to bridge that unbridgeable gap between man and God by becoming man Yourself through Your Son, Jesus Christ! Amen.

No one ... was able to open the book or to look in it. Here is a paradox: the book is meant for mankind, but no man can open it. Yet God requires someone to open it. Who will solve this mystery?

March 8 – Revelation 5:4

And I wept much, because no man was found worthy to open and to read the book, neither to look thereon.

Why did John weep?

Why was this so important to John?

How is this weeping tied to the commission Jesus gave him in Revelation 1:1-3?

Prayer: Holy Father, when all hope is lost when we are in impossible circumstances from which there is no escape, we still have hope in You. You are the God of the impossible, which You have done and will continue to do, forever. We praise You in Jesus's Name. Amen.

And I wept much – Revelation 1:1-2 *This is the Revelation of Jesus Christ, which God gave him to show to his servants the things which must happen soon, which he sent and made known by his angel to his servant, John,[2] who testified to God's word and of the testimony of Jesus Christ, about everything that he saw.*

The book contains Jesus's commission to John.

Revelation 1:11 *"What you see, write in a book and send to the seven assemblies: to Ephesus, Smyrna, Pergamum, Thyatira, Sardis, Philadelphia, and to Laodicea."*

So, with the book sealed, John could not see what was in the book and could not complete his commission.

March 9 – Revelation 5:5

One of the elders said to me, "Don't weep. Behold, the Lion who is of the tribe of Judah, the Root of David, has overcome: he who opens the book and its seven seals."

Who is the Lion of Judah?

Who is the Root of David?

How did He prevail to open the book and break the seals?

Prayer: Thank You, Lord Jesus, that You prevailed and overcame sin and death while You were a man. You were our sin-bearer. You are our Redeemer, buying us back from sin and death by paying the price in Your flesh—our very Creator dying for us. You defeated Satan forever, and we rejoice in Your triumph. Amen.

"The Lion who is of the tribe of Judah, the Root of David." The phrase "Lion of the tribe of Judah" only occurs here. But Judah and a lion are linked in this prophecy:

Hosea 5:14 *For I will be to Ephraim like a lion, and like a young lion to the house of Judah. I myself will tear in pieces and go away. I will carry off, and there will be no one to deliver.*

This is the Lord God speaking, prophesying the future captivity of Ephraim and Judah. He calls Himself a lion. Therefore, the Lion of Judah is God.

The Root of David is defined within the book of Revelation:

Revelation 22:16 *"I, Jesus, have sent my angel to testify these things to you for the assemblies. I am the root and the offspring of David, the Bright and Morning Star."*

Jesus is the root of David.

March 10 – Revelation 5:6

And I beheld, and, lo, in the midst of the throne and of the four beasts, and in the midst of the elders, stood a Lamb as it had been slain, having seven horns and seven eyes, which are the seven Spirits of God sent forth into all the earth

Who is the Lamb Who was slain?

What do the seven eyes of the Lamb mean?

How do the seven eyes of the Lamb serve Him?

Prayer: Ah, mighty God, holy King of the universe, help us to realize nothing we do is hidden from you, but all our deeds and thoughts are before You. Thus Your judgment of us is perfect, knowing all our motivations and thoughts more clearly than we do ourselves. Help us to use this knowledge to submit to Your will more completely. In Jesus's Name, we pray. Amen.

Seven eyes, which are the seven Spirits of God sent forth into all the earth. We already encountered the sevenfold Spirit of God in **Revelation 4**, symbolized by the seven lamps before the throne of God. The lamp flames and the eyes are linked in Zechariah.

Zechariah 4:2, 10 *He said to me, "What do you see?" I said, "I have seen, and behold, a lamp stand all of gold, with its bowl on the top of it, and its seven lamps on it; there are seven pipes to each of the lamps, which are on the top of it;[10] Indeed, who despises the day of small things? For these seven shall rejoice, and shall see the plumb line in the hand of Zerubbabel. These are Yahweh's eyes, which run back and forth through the whole earth."*

In the Trinity, the sevenfold Spirit serves as God's eyes upon the earth.

March 11 – Revelation 5:7

Then He came, and He took it out of the right hand of Him who sat on the throne.

Who took the book from the right hand of God?

Where is the transfer of knowledge previously mentioned in the book of Revelation?

What will the Lamb of God do with the book?

Prayer: Holy Father, thank You for revealing mysteries to Your servants through Jesus Christ the Revelator. Such truth comes from You and encourages us in our battles on this earth. Thank You for Your love. Amen.

This is the Revelation of Jesus Christ, which God gave him to show to his servants the things which must happen soon. The first verse of the book of Revelation is revealed here. John sees what happened behind the scenes before his vision began.

March 12 - Revelation 5:8

Now when he had taken the book, the four living creatures and the twenty-four elders fell down before the Lamb, each one having a harp, and golden bowls full of incense, which are the prayers of the saints.

What did the twenty-four elders do after the Lamb took the book?

What do the twenty-four elders have?

1.

2.

Why are bowls of incense appropriate for the elders to have?

Prayer: Father in heaven, we, too, join in worshipping You today for Your marvelous wisdom. Not only do You accomplish the impossible — the salvation of mankind — but You teach and reveal Your work in wonderful ways. Amen.

Each one having a harp, and golden bowls full of incense. The twenty-four elders are symbolized by the ancient Israelite priesthood, with its twenty-four courses of priests. In **1 Chronicles 24**, they present incense in the Temple. The next chapter, **1 Chronicles 25**, tells of the twenty-four courses of worship leaders who were to praise God with harps. Thus the temple service pictured God's liturgical service in heaven.

March 13 – Revelation 5:9

They sang a new song, saying, "You are worthy to take the book and to open its seals: for you were killed, and bought them for God with your blood out of every tribe, language, people, and nation."

What did the twenty-four elders do?

To Whom did they sing their new song?

When do they sing?

Why did they sing their song?

Prayer: Holy Father, the salvation You wrought through Your Son, Jesus, is so remarkable we can only burst out in song in response. You bought every human being back from sin and death by Jesus's blood, if we only believe. You also give us the faith to believe. Who can stop praising You? In the Name of our Savior, we pray. Amen.

"Out of every tribe, language, people, and nation." Salvation is universally offered, but it's not universally accepted. Peter makes it clear that only through faith in Jesus Christ can we be saved. In **Acts 4:12**, Paul states that our faith itself is a gift from God. And according to **Ephesians 2:8**, our whole salvation is a gift. Oddly, some people still refuse to be saved.

March 14 - Revelation 5:10

"You made them kings and priests to our God, and they will reign on the earth." (Holman Christian Standard Bible)

What is the future of mankind? What will we become?

1.

2.

Where will we rule?

Who makes this future come to pass?

When will this happen?

Prayer: Thank You, Father, for fulfilling Your purpose for humanity through Jesus Christ, our Savior, Lord, and King. You intended to dwell with men and women in Eden while we ruled the Earth forever. Our sin separated us from You, but You healed the breach through Jesus Christ. Glory to You forever. Amen.

"You made them kings and priests to our God." "Them" refers back to "every tribe, tongue, people, and nation" in the previous verse. God's will and plan from the beginning is for mankind to rule the earth with Him. Although man sinned, neither His will nor His plan failed, thanks to Jesus coming as a sacrifice for all mankind's sins.

March 15 – Revelation 5:11

I saw, and I heard something like a voice of many angels around the throne, the living creatures, and the elders. The number of them was ten thousands of ten thousands, and thousands of thousands.

Who is praising?

Where are they praising?

What is the rough number of those praising?

Prayer: O magnificent Father, we have been thrilled by awesome music at times in our lives, but the music of Your praise is the greatest of all. Let us add our little human voices each day as we praise You in prayer with all of our hearts. In the mighty Name of Jesus, we worship You. Amen.

I heard the voice of many angels round about the throne. We rarely think about the myriads of angels working for God as He rules the universe. They attend to His business on Earth and carry our prayers back to His throne. Here we have a glimpse of their mass worship, with hundreds of millions of angels of all types around His throne as the Lamb unseals the scroll.

March 16 – Revelation 5:12

Saying with a loud voice, "Worthy is the Lamb who has been killed to receive the power, wealth, wisdom, strength, honor, glory, and blessing!"

What do the angels say?

What is the Lamb worthy to receive?

1.

2.

3.

4.

5.

6.

7.

Prayer: O Holy Father, the Lamb is so worthy and so glorious that only by listing the traits of His greatness can we grasp how great He is. Wonderful Jesus, let us praise You every day for another of Your marvelous characteristics. In Your Name, we pray. Amen.

Saying with a loud voice. We're used to shouting for celebrities and sports champions in this world. How much more so should we cheer for the ultimate Victor over sin and death, Jesus Christ? He solved Adam's first sin. Through Jesus, the world will not merely return to the Edenic paradise God envisioned but transcend it greatly into a universal, everlasting paradise where God and man dwell in harmony forever.

March 17 – Revelation 5:13

I heard every created thing which is in heaven, on the earth, under the earth, on the sea, and everything in them, saying, "To him who sits on the throne, and to the Lamb be the blessing, the honor, the glory, and the dominion, forever and ever! Amen!"

Who is praising God and the Lamb?

How is this group different from the group in verse 5:11?

What do they say?

1.

2.

3.

4.

Prayer: O glorious God, the praise of all of heaven is not enough for You and the Lamb. We add our praise, from all mankind and all Your creation here on Earth, under the Earth, and in the air of heaven. We bless You with all our hearts, for all blessings come from You—past, present, and future, forever. In Jesus's Name, we pray. Amen.

Every created thing which is in heaven, on the earth, under the earth, on the sea, and everything in them. This praise comes from not only all of mankind but all creatures of any sort in the whole environment of the Earth. This is voluntary praise, spontaneous and heartfelt, for Jesus reigns, and all stories on the Earth will end well.

March 18 – Revelation 5:14

The four living creatures said, "Amen!" Then the twenty-four elders fell down and worshiped the one living forever and ever.

What did the four beasts/creatures/seraphim do?

What did the twenty-four elders do?

What were the seraphim saying Amen to?

Prayer: – O Father, You unite heaven and Earth in praise and worship of Your Son, Jesus Christ. You are right and just to exalt Your Son for no other act of bravery and love is comparable to His sacrifice, which saved all of mankind and the whole universe from sin. Glory to God forever for Your unimaginable love and audacious plan of salvation. Amen.

And the four beasts said, "Amen!" The four seraphim next to God's throne agreed with the praise of all the creatures of the Earth in the previous verse.

Revelation 5:13 *"To him who sits on the throne, and to the Lamb be the blessing, the honor, the glory, and the dominion, forever and ever!"* God thus unites creatures of heaven and Earth in praise of the Lamb.

March 19 - Revelation 6:1

I saw that the Lamb opened one of the seven seals, and I heard one of the four living creatures saying, as with a voice of thunder, "Come and see!"

What happened when the Lamb opened the first seal?

1.

2.

Who was invited to come and see?

Where were these seals opened in John's vision?

Prayer: Father, we praise You that through Jesus Christ we may have access to the greatest secrets of heaven. These things the angels did not know until You revealed them through Jesus the Revelator. Then through John, You revealed them to us. Help us to hear and to act on this knowledge from the throne of God. In Jesus's Name, we pray. Amen.

Saying, as with a voice of thunder. This sound of thunder seems to be a minor detail, but this sound is all through Revelation and around God's throne. Consider lightning and thunder first appeared when God came down on Mount Sinai in **Exodus 19**. Observe the other places thunder occurs in Revelation.

March 20 – Revelation 6:2

And I saw, and behold a white horse: and he that sat on him had a bow; and a crown was given unto him: and he went forth conquering, and to conquer.

What did John see?

1.

2.

3.

What did the horseman do?

Prayer: All praise to You, Holy Father, and to Jesus our Revelator! You tell us what will happen before it happens. Thank You, Jesus, for not only revealing the future to us in Revelation but also in the gospels. Thank You for staying with Your church to the very end of the age and sustaining us through all persecution. Glory to You forever for Your triumph in the church! Amen.

A white horse: and he that sat on him had a bow; and a crown. Some have thought this was a picture of Jesus.

Yet in **Revelation 19:11-12** *I saw the heaven opened, and behold, a white horse, and he who sat on it is called Faithful and True. In righteousness he judges and makes war.[12] His eyes are a flame of fire, and on his head are many crowns.*

Jesus is portrayed on a white horse with many crowns. **Revelation 19** takes place after His second coming. His second coming has not yet been mentioned in **Revelation 6**. Who can solve this mystery? Jesus Himself gives the future to the disciples.

Matthew 24:3-5 *As he sat on the Mount of Olives, the disciples came to him privately, saying, "Tell us, when will these things be? What is the sign of your coming, and of the end of the age?"[4] Jesus answered them, "Be careful that no one leads you astray.[5] For many will come* *in my name, saying, 'I am the Christ,' and will lead many astray"*.

The first thing Jesus mentions are false messiahs, and the first seal is someone who looks like Jesus but is not.

March 21 – Revelation 6:3-4

When he opened the second seal, I heard the second living creature saying, "Come!"[4] Another came out: a red horse. To him who sat on it was given power to take peace from the earth, and that they should kill one another. There was given to him a great sword.

Who announces the second seal?

What appears with the second seal?

1.

2.

3.

4.

Prayer: O Prince of Peace, come quickly! O Yahweh Shalom, come and bring peace, for it has been taken from the Earth in our lifetimes and our history since the days of Jesus. Make us the instruments of Your peace, bringing it wherever we may go. O come quickly, Lord Jesus. Amen

It was given power to take peace from the earth, and that they should kill one another. The second horseman of the Apocalypse (Revelation) takes peace from the Earth. Since Jesus's day, there have been many wars and much death. What did Jesus say about this in His earlier prophecy? [11]

Matthew 24:6-7 *You will hear of wars and rumors of wars. See that you aren't troubled, for all this must happen, but the end is not yet.[7] For nation will rise against nation, and kingdom against kingdom; and there will be famines, plagues, and earthquakes in various places.*

Mark 13:7 *"When you hear of wars and rumors of wars, don't be troubled. For those must happen, but the end is not yet."*

Luke 21:9 *"When you hear of wars and disturbances, don't be terrified, for these things must happen first, but the end won't come immediately."*

March 22 – Revelation 6:5-6

When he opened the third seal, I heard the third living creature saying, "Come and see!" And behold, a black horse, and he who sat on it had a balance in his hand.[6] I heard a voice in the middle of the four living creatures saying, "A choenix (quart or liter) of wheat for a denarius, and three choenix of barley for a denarius! Don't damage the oil and the wine!"

Who speaks to John?

What did the rider of the third horse have?

What did the voice amid the four creatures say?

What do you think the third horseman represents?

Prayer: Father in heaven, we've had famines since the time of Jesus, and they will continue until His return. Let us remember to look to You for our daily bread. And more, let us look to Jesus as our daily Bread of Life. In His Name, we pray. Amen.

"(quart or liter) of wheat for a denarius." A denarius was the average daily wage in John's time. Jesus cited this in His parable of the workers in the vineyard. As I write this in 2023, the wheat cost is per 1 Kilogram is $1.00. USD.[14]

A kilogram is about a quart of wheat. What's a day's wage today? At a minimum wage of $15/hour, 8 hours of work is $120.[8] This would be a stupendous cost for wheat, which can happen during a famine.

March 23 – Revelation 6:7-8

When he opened the fourth seal, I heard the fourth living creature saying, "Come and see!"[8] And behold, a pale horse, and the name of he who sat on it was Death. Hades followed with him. Authority over one fourth of the earth, to kill with the sword, with famine, with death, and by the wild animals of the earth was given to him.

What was the name of the fourth horseman?

What authority was given to him?

How would he exercise this authority?

What is the current population of the Earth? What is a quarter of that?

Prayer: Father, truly terrible times are coming. Help us to stay with You through these times, for we know You will stay with us. We have Jesus's promise, "I'll never leave nor forsake you." In His Name, we pray. Amen.

To kill with the sword, with famine, with death, and by the wild animals of the earth. In our current world, we don't fear wild animals, for they can be killed by firearms. However, if society breaks down, the animals will multiply, particularly the predators. Without a working civilization, ammunition will run out, and wild animals will become a deadly threat.

March 24 – Revelation 6:9

When he opened the fifth seal, I saw underneath the altar the souls of those who had been killed for the Word of God, and for the testimony of the Lamb which they had.

Whom does John see after the fifth seal is broken?

Where are these souls?

Why had they been killed?

Prayer: O Lord God, You say the death of Your saints is precious in Your sight. You gave Your life for ours, and our lives are Yours. Let us gladly give up our lives for You. Strengthen us for the hour of trial and testing. In Jesus's Name, we pray. Amen.

Underneath the altar the souls of those who had been killed for the Word of God. Can you imagine people being killed for the Word of God, the Bible? It happens daily in our world where the Bible and Christianity are forbidden. There are dozens of countries where Christianity is forbidden. The martyrs are also killed for testifying about Jesus and how He changed their lives. These souls are precious to God, and they are next to God's altar in heaven, where incense of prayers to God are offered.

March 25 - Revelation 6:10

And they cried with a loud voice, saying, "How long, O Lord, holy and true, dost thou not judge and avenge our blood on them that dwell on the earth?

What do the martyrs for Christ say to God?

Why does God allow His followers to be martyred?

Why haven't the martyrs been avenged by God?

Prayer: O Father, we don't know why some people are spared from death and others are not. But we do know You are a just God, and nothing escapes Your knowledge. We also know You have infinite knowledge of all people and circumstances—past, present, and future—and all things will work out according to Your good will. Help us to be patient and trust in You. In Jesus's Name, Who trusted in You to death, we pray. Amen.

How long, O Lord, holy and true. Thus men and women have prayed since the beginning. We have faced sorrow and evil since the days of Adam and Eve, and thousands of years seem like forever to endure injustice and crime. But God sees and perceives years by the billion, and His plans extend to infinity. God does not explain Himself but leaves us to trust Him in His goodness, shown by Jesus on the cross.

March 26 – Revelation 6:11

A long white robe was given to each of them. They were told that they should rest yet for a while, until their fellow servants and their brothers, who would also be killed even as they were, should complete their course.

How long were they told to rest?

What was given to them?

What does the gift represent?

Prayer: Father in heaven, help us look past our current sufferings, even persecution and death, to the eternal reward You have for each son and daughter of Yours who suffers and dies as did Your own Son, Jesus Christ. Help us to keep our eyes focused on Jesus, our pioneer in death and life eternal. Amen.

Until their fellow servants and their brothers, who would also be killed. Devotees of end-time prophesy rarely quote this prophecy of a future martyrdom of Christians. But all Christians should be mentally prepared to give up their lives for God. Jesus prophesied in the gospels:[11]

Matthew 24:9-12, 21 *"Then they will deliver you up to oppression and will kill you. You will be hated by all of the nations for my name's sake.[10] Then many will stumble, and will deliver up one another, and will hate one another.[11] Many false prophets will arise and will lead many astray.[12] Because iniquity will be multiplied, the love of many will grow cold.[21] for then there will be great suffering such as has not been from the beginning of the world until now, no, nor ever will be.*

Mark 13:9, 19 *But watch yourselves, for they will deliver you up to councils. You will be beaten in synagogues. You will stand before rulers and kings for my sake, for a testimony to them[19] For in those days there will be oppression, such as there has not been the like from the beginning of the creation which God created until now, and never will be.*

Luke 21:12 *But before all these things, they will lay their hands on you and will persecute you, delivering you up to synagogues and prisons, bringing you before kings and governors for my name's sake.*

March 27 – Revelation 6:12

I saw when he opened the sixth seal, and there was a great earthquake. The sun became black as sackcloth made of hair, and the whole moon became as blood.

What were the first three things to happen with the sixth seal?

1.

2.

3.

How long would these three events take?

Prayer: O Father, help us to fear You and our coming, King Jesus Christ, but not the disasters that happen around us. The world has shed innocent blood and must be punished. Save us out of these things. In Jesus's Name, we pray. Amen.

There was a great earthquake. This is the first of five earthquakes cited in the book of Revelation. There have been earthquakes since Jesus's day, some very great indeed. Yet these five are distinctive because they marked changes in the prophecy of Revelation. Here, within the seven seals, the earthquake marks the beginning of heavenly signs and God's direct intervention in the world.

March 28 – Revelation 6:13

The stars of the sky fell to the earth, like a fig tree dropping its unripe figs when it is shaken by a great wind.

What do you think these falling stars mean?

How many figs or other fruit are shed by trees in a hurricane?

Have you ever seen shooting stars so thick they look like fruit blown in a windstorm?

Prayer: Father, we thank You for giving mankind clear signs of Your intervention on earth, so that even people ignorant of this prophecy will realize You are personally intervening in the affairs of mankind. In the Name of King Jesus, we're grateful. Amen.

And the stars of heaven fell unto the earth. Just as we understand today, John and his audience realized shooting stars are not stars as we see in the constellations, but, instead, meteors which may hit the Earth and leave pieces of metal behind. Shooting stars may be seen most nights. To be used as a sign, the meteor shower must be especially thick and long-lasting, possibly impacting civilization with heavy damage.

March 29 – Revelation 6:14

And the heaven departed as a scroll when it is rolled together; and every mountain and island were moved out of their places.

What is the perspective for this verse, from Earth or heaven?

What does a scroll look like as it's rolled up? How can the sky look like this?

What is the scope of the earthquake mentioned in Revelation 6:12?

Prayer: O help us hear Your Word, holy Father! Let us not be so dense and stubborn that we ignore You until the world itself begins to shake all around us and the sky disappears! Help us repent now! In Jesus's Name, we pray. Amen.

Every mountain and island were moved out of their places. Earthquakes often move entire mountains, islands, and coastlines many feet. Here God causes an earthquake that does this to every mountain and island. Will mankind begin to listen to Him? Will we listen now?

March 30 – Revelation 6:15

The kings of the earth, the princes, the commanding officers, the rich, the strong, and every slave and free person, hid themselves in the caves and in the rocks of the mountains.

Who is mentioned in this verse?

1.

2.

3.

4.

5.

6.

7.

What did they all do?

Why?

Prayer: Father in heaven, help us to fear You every day, not just when our life is threatened by some disaster. You are awesome beyond the universe, and yet You love us so intensely You won't let us remain in sin. You give us the choice between sin and death and righteousness and eternal life in Jesus Christ. We choose You, Most High God! Amen.

Hid themselves in the dens and in the rocks of the mountains. The heavenly signs, the tremendous meteor shower, and the sky being rolled away scare every person of all social statuses, and all hide underground.

March 31 – Revelation 6:16

They told the mountains and the rocks, "Fall on us, and hide us from the face of him who sits on the throne, and from the wrath of the Lamb,

Why is humanity hiding underground?

Why are they afraid of the Father on the throne and the Lamb of God?

What is the danger of hiding underground?

Prayer: O God, when the day of Your wrath comes, help us to stand tall and face You unafraid, knowing that all our sins are forgiven in Jesus Christ our Lord. Help us always remember that there is no condemnation for those who are in Christ Jesus. In His Name, we pray. Amen.

"Fall on us, and hide us." So great is the terror of mankind facing the judgment day of God that the vast majority hide underground rather than face the terror of God's coming in the sky. This is a substantial risk since the world just experienced a stupendous worldwide earthquake, and there are dangers of aftershocks and cave-ins.

April 1 – Revelation 6:17

"For the great day of his wrath has come; and who is able to stand?"

What does all mankind know is coming?

How do they know this?

Why do they fear God?

Prayer: Father in heaven, You are holy, and we fear You now. Even as Your children, we know Your position and authority over us. Let us always look to Jesus as our perfect example and copy Him every day of our lives. In His Name, we pray, Amen.

"For the great day of his wrath is come." The whole world knows God is returning to judge the world. How do they know, since the vast majority are non-Christian? 1) There was a worldwide earthquake that had never happened before; 2) There were heavenly signs and an awesome meteor shower; 3) The sky rolled away. The image of what this looks like isn't clear, but perhaps heaven, and God's throne, are revealed. 4) There is the preaching of the two witnesses of God. (See **Revelation 11**.)

April 2 - Revelation 7:1

After this, I saw four angels standing at the four corners of the earth, holding the four winds of the earth, so that no wind would blow on the earth, or on the sea, or on any tree.

What is John's perspective in this vision?

Why are the angels holding the four winds of the Earth?

What do the four corners of the Earth mean?

Prayer: Father in heaven, help us understand each verse in the Bible and the book of Revelation so we may understand Your perspective. With the insight of Your view, let us live our lives so that we please You and Jesus Christ today. Amen.

Four angels standing at the four corners of the earth. Traditionally, the four corners of the Earth and the four winds are North, South, East, and West. The angels are restraining the winds for God's purpose. It will soon be revealed in the next verses.

April 3 – Revelation 7:2

And I saw another angel ascending from the east, having the seal of the living God: and he cried with a loud voice to the four angels, to whom it was given to hurt the earth and the sea.

Who are the four angels to whom it is given to hurt the earth and sea? Are these the same ones holding back the winds?

What is the seal of the living God?

Is coming from the east significant?

Prayer: Father, You weave so many symbols and meanings together in the Bible that our heads spin. Yet You want us to work to understand Your word, for then we appreciate the meaning more. Help us to humbly seek Your truth and recognize it when we find it. In Jesus's Name, we pray the Word of God. Amen.

Having the seal of the living God. This symbol of a seal has a clear meaning in Scripture:

Ephesians 1:13 *In Him you also, having heard the word of the truth, the Good News of your salvation – in whom, having also believed, you were sealed with the promised Holy Spirit.*

Ephesians 4:30 *Don't grieve the Holy Spirit of God, in whom you were sealed for the day of redemption.*

2 Corinthians 1:21-22 *Now he who establishes us with you in Christ and anointed us is God,[22] who also sealed us, and gave us the down payment of the Spirit in our hearts.*

April 4 – Revelation 7:3

Saying, Hurt not the earth, neither the sea, nor the trees, till we have sealed the servants of our God in their foreheads.

What is the purpose of this sealing?

Who is sealed?

Who are the servants of God?

Prayer: Our Father in heaven, help us to be good servants of Yours, as well as Your sons and daughters. We have Your seal of approval and our guarantee of salvation since we first trusted in Christ to save us. Help us live up to Your approval. In Jesus's Name, we pray. Amen.

Till we have sealed the servants of our God in their foreheads. Ezekiel also shows a marking of God's people in the forehead:

Ezekiel 9:4 *Yahweh said to him, "Go through the middle of the city, through the middle of Jerusalem, and set a mark on the foreheads of the men that sigh and that cry over all the abominations that are done within it."*

This is set before the destruction of Jerusalem. The sealing of **Revelation 7** is worldwide and before God strikes the whole Earth.

April 5 – Revelation 7:4

I heard the number of those who were sealed, one hundred forty-four thousand, sealed out of every tribe of the children of Israel.

What did John hear?

Who was sealed?

How many were sealed?

Prayer: Father, we look to You to save us and seal us in Your power. Help us to love everyone as Jesus did. In His Name, we pray. Amen

I heard the number of those who were sealed. The phrase "I heard" was used with each of the first four seals, but not with the next two. Now John hears the number of those sealed rather like the censuses of Israel in Numbers before and after the forty years in the wilderness. We'll read more about this number tomorrow.

April 6 – Revelation 7:5-8

of the tribe of Judah twelve thousand were sealed,
of the tribe of Reuben twelve thousand,
of the tribe of Gad twelve thousand,
⁶ of the tribe of Asher twelve thousand,
of the tribe of Naphtali twelve thousand,
of the tribe of Manasseh twelve thousand,
⁷ of the tribe of Simeon twelve thousand,
of the tribe of Levi twelve thousand,
of the tribe of Issachar twelve thousand,
⁸ of the tribe of Zebulun twelve thousand,
of the tribe of Joseph twelve thousand, and
of the tribe of Benjamin twelve thousand were sealed.

How many tribes were sealed?

Which tribe isn't mentioned?

Which tribe is mentioned that isn't usually counted?

Prayer: Father, thank you for posing mysteries for us so we may dig more deeply into Your Word. Even with the best of our efforts, we don't understand everything. Help us to wait patiently until You reveal all things in Your time. In Jesus's Name, we pray. Amen.

Of the tribe of Joseph twelve thousand. Oddly, Joseph had not been counted as a tribe since **Genesis 46**. In **Genesis 48** Israel blessed and adopted Joseph's two sons, Ephraim and Manasseh, as his own, and they took the place of Joseph's tribe. In the censuses of **Numbers (1 and 26)**, Ephraim and Manasseh each were counted as separate tribes. If we take Joseph as Ephraim, this count fits. However, Levi was treated specially as the priestly tribe and not counted among the twelve tribes. Further, the tribe of Dan is missing altogether. The Bible doesn't explain these mysteries.

April 7 – Revelation 7:9

After these things I looked, and behold, a great multitude, which no man could count, out of every nation and of all tribes, peoples, and languages, standing before the throne and before the Lamb, dressed in white robes, with palm branches in their hands.

Who did John see, as opposed to what he heard?

What was John's perspective as he beheld them?

What do the white robes represent?

Prayer: Father God, help us through Jesus Christ to be thoroughly clean and be worthy to stand before You in the Presence of the Lamb Who saves us. Amen.

a great multitude, . . . of all nations, and kindreds, and people, and tongues. This phrase covers every nation, race, and language—every people group that exists or has ever existed. Further, this multitude is all saved by Jesus and standing before God's throne in heaven. Who are they? See the verses over the next few days.

April 8 – Revelation 7:10

They cried with a loud voice, saying, "Salvation be to our God, who sits on the throne, and to the Lamb!"

What does the innumerable multitude say?

What do these words indicate?

What other part of the Bible has cries of "Hosanna" (He saves) to Jesus?

Prayer: Hosanna! Salvation belongs to You, God, and the Lamb, Jesus Christ. We welcome You now into our hearts, minds, and lives as our King. Expand Your Kingdom over the whole world and the entire universe! In Jesus's Name, we pray. Amen.

Salvation to our God . . . and unto the Lamb. All four gospels record Jesus's entry into Jerusalem before the Passover festival. People praised Him as He descended from the Mount of Olives on a donkey's foal and as He entered Jerusalem.

April 9 – Revelation 7:11

All the angels were standing around the throne, the elders, and the four living creatures; and they fell on their faces before his throne, and worshiped God.

What is the response of heaven to the innumerable multitude?

Who is worshipping God in heaven?

Where were they worshipping?

Prayer: Father, if these powerful heavenly beings You have created humble themselves and worship You, how much more should we, men and women of the Earth, made of the dust of the ground, worship You? Let us never be prideful, but humble before You every day. In the Name of the Lamb of God, we pray, Amen.

All the angels were standing around the throne. We know there were multiple hundreds of millions from **Revelation 5:11.** This leads to more questions: How did they all hear? How did they all see? How were they all coordinated in their worship? There is so much we do not know.

April 10 – Revelation 7:12

Saying, "Amen! Blessing, glory, wisdom, thanksgiving, honor, power, and might, be to our God forever and ever! Amen."

What does all of heaven say together?

Why are they praising God?

What are they feeling at this time?

Prayer: Father, we give You our wholehearted praise. Let us hold nothing back, for You are great and deserve more than we can give. In the Name of our Savior, we pray. Amen.

"Blessing, glory, wisdom, thanksgiving, honor, power, and might, be to our God forever and ever!" This appears to be a praise chorus, which all of heaven knows. Who can imagine the colossal sound they create around the throne?

April 11 - Revelation 7:13-14

One of the elders answered, saying to me, "These who are arrayed in the white robes, who are they, and where did they come from?"[14] I told him, "My lord, you know."

He said to me, "These are those who came out of the great suffering. They washed their robes, and made them white in the Lamb's blood."

Why did the elder ask John if he knew about the multitude?

Who are the multitude?

Where did they come from?

What have they done?

Prayer: Father, we never thought we were worthy to enter Your Presence like this multitude. Yet You called us and have washed us in the blood of the Lamb. Help us and all my brethren finish the race You have set before us, regardless of what happens. In Jesus's Name, we pray. Amen.

These are they which came out of great suffering. Remember the fifth seal? The martyrs were waiting in white robes for the rest of their brethren to be killed as they were. **Revelation 6:11** shows this event has happened on Earth.

April 12 - Revelation 7:15

Therefore they are before the throne of God, they serve him day and night in his temple. He who sits on the throne will spread his tabernacle over them.

Where are the innumerable multitude?

What does the innumerable multitude do?

Who will dwell with the innumerable multitude?

Prayer: O God, help us to serve You in Your temple now, today, in Your church. Let us not shrink from any task You give us, big or small. In Jesus's Name, the humble Servant, we pray. Amen.

They serve him day and night in his temple. We often think of this service as in the future and heaven. Yet God is timeless, and He is omnipresent. We are before Him on the Earth, and if we are in His Church, we are currently in His temple. What opportunities do we have to serve? How are we serving now?

April 13 – Revelation 7:16

They will never be hungry or thirsty any more. The sun won't beat on them, nor any heat.

What will happen to the innumerable multitude?

What does it mean to never be hungry or thirsty any more?

What does it mean to be impervious to heat?

Prayer: Father, thank You for Your protection from heat and cold, hunger and thirst, and even death. You provide for all our needs, even eternal life, through our Savior Jesus Christ. What more can You give? Everything else is icing on the cake. Praise to You forever. Amen.

They will never be hungry or thirsty any more. These are daily needs we have in our physical body. Will we not need to eat in our spiritual body? Jesus ate with His disciples twice or more after His resurrection. We certainly can eat, but as Jesus spoke of the Spirit welling up as a fountain in each of us, we will never need water again.

John 4:14 *God is our all-sufficient sustenance.*

April 14 – Revelation 7:17

For the Lamb who is in the middle of the throne shepherds them and leads them to springs of life-giving waters. And God will wipe away every tear from their eyes.

What will the Lamb do for the innumerable multitude?

What does it mean for God to wipe away every tear from every eye?

What do these springs of water mean or symbolize?

How can Jesus be both a Lamb and a Shepherd?

Prayer: O holy God, You can do all things. You sacrificed Your Son and brought Him back to life, all with perfect justice. Jesus, You led Your people Israel, and when they rebelled, You died in their place. You opened the door for the Spirit to enter each of us, giving us a new heart and mind, making all things new. You are our Creator, physically and spiritually, and we are Your children. All praise we have, all we have, goes to You. Amen.

God will wipe away every tear from their eyes. Think about this. God touches our cheeks, and our eyes, and wipes away our tears. Think of how gentle He is, how intimate He is, how knowing He is, to comfort exactly what grieves us. Think of how powerful He is to make all our griefs vanish along with all our tears. There will be no grief in His Kingdom.

April 15 – Revelation 8:1

When he opened the seventh seal, there was silence in heaven for about half an hour.

What happens at the seventh seal?

How is this different from the other six seals?

What do you think the silence signifies?

Prayer: Father, all You do is awesome, yet the seventh seal seems especially so, for there is silence even in heaven for half an hour. All of heaven and all of Earth hold their breath for what comes next. You are our God of supreme surprises and twists in reality, all to accomplish Your will. We praise You forever in Jesus's Name. Amen.

Silence in heaven for about half an hour. Remember, the four creatures, the seraphim, are continually praising God. They fall silent. The twenty-four elders, God's priestly council, fall silent instead of casting their crowns and praising God. Even the thunder and lightning about the throne of God fall silent. Silence can be the best emphasis for what happens next.

April 16 – Revelation 8:2

And I saw the seven angels which stood before God; and to them were given seven trumpets.

What is the significance of angels standing before God?

What is the significance of trumpets in the Bible?

What is the significance of "seven" in the Bible?

Prayer: Father, help us to fear to disobey You in our daily lives. You are exceedingly gracious and merciful, giving all mankind time to repent. But when the time of mercy runs out, You are utterly fearful in Your wrath. Help us to preach Your gospel now before it is too late. In Jesus's Name, we pray. Amen.

Seven angels who stood before God. To stand before God is a great honor, both for men and angels. Note what the angel Gabriel says to Zacharias the priest:

Luke 1:19-20 *The angel answered him, "I am Gabriel, who stands in the presence of God. I was sent to speak to you and to bring you this good news.*[20] *Behold, you will be silent and not able to speak until the day that these things will happen, because you didn't believe my words, which will be fulfilled in their proper time."*

Gabriel, who brought the news of John the Baptist's and Jesus's births, is one angel who stands before God. He has the authority to bring judgment on Zacharias for his unbelief. What authority will be given to these seven angels?

April 17 – Revelation 8:3

And another angel came and stood at the altar, having a golden censer; and there was given unto him much incense, that he should offer it with the prayers of all saints upon the golden altar which was before the throne.

Where was the altar of incense in the tabernacle and the temple?

Where is the altar of incense located in heaven?

What is offered with incense on the altar in heaven?

Prayer: O God in heaven, let us never fail to offer You our prayers each day. How can we stop giving you homage and praise? How can we stop, knowing you have each prayer brought before Your throne by a powerful angel and You examine each one? Fill us up with zeal for You so our prayers burn with our passion. In Jesus's Name, we pray. Amen.

He should offer it with the prayers of all saints upon the golden altar which was before the throne. In the temple and the tabernacle, the priest's duty was to offer incense each day at the incense altar. This golden altar was just outside the veil of the Most Holy Place and filled the whole interior with smoke and scent. How important was this act?

Leviticus 16:13 *He shall put the incense on the fire before Yahweh, that the cloud of the incense may cover the mercy seat that is on the covenant so that he will not die.*

The high priest himself could be killed by God if he approached the mercy seat (the throne of God, the covering of the Ark of the Covenant) without incense.

Although God is bringing judgment on the Earth, the prayers of the saints are bringing mercy and life.

April 18 – Revelation 8:4

The smoke of the incense, with the prayers of the saints, went up before God out of the angel's hand.

What ascended before God from the angel's hand?

1.

2.

What role is the angel performing in heaven?

Is this role unique to this time or is it repeated?

Prayer: Thank You, Father, that You consider our prayer sacred enough to come into Your Presence and that they are sweet to You, as incense is. You are sweet to us, Almighty God. You are beautiful and fragrant and love us dearly. Amen.

Went up before God out of the angel's hand. Revelation is a unique book of prophecy, the only one in the New Testament. It is full of images and actions that are found nowhere else in Scripture. The whole sequence of the seven seals and their results are only found here. It would not be surprising if the angel's work as a priest was unique and preparatory to the results of the seventh seal.

April 19 – Revelation 8:5

The angel took the censer, and he filled it with the fire of the altar, then threw it on the earth. Thunders, sounds, lightnings, and an earthquake followed.

What three things did the angel do?

1.

2.

3.

What were the four results of the angel's actions?

1.

2.

3.

4.

How many earthquakes is this so far?

Prayer: Father in heaven, we pray for Your kingdom to come, but we can't imagine the full immensity of the terror that will come to the Earth. Millennia of injustice and evil, bloody crimes, and wars are heaped upon the Earth and cry out for judgment. Help us to remain true to You and not be influenced by society around us. We rest and hope in Jesus, our Lord. Amen.

Thunders, sounds, lightnings, and an earthquake followed. This is the second earthquake mentioned: one after the sixth seal and one after the seventh seal. The sixth seal began God's intervention on the Earth, and the seventh seal continues and completes it.

April 20 – Revelation 8:6-7

The seven angels who had the seven trumpets prepared themselves to sound.[7] The first sounded, and there followed hail and fire, mixed with blood, and they were thrown to the earth. One third of the earth was burned up, and one third of the trees were burned up, and all green grass was burned up.

Why did the angels have to prepare themselves to blow trumpets?

What would be the effect of burning one-third of all vegetation on the Earth?

What would mankind do in response?

Prayer: Father, mankind has been destroying the good Earth You created for millennia. Now You take away some of what You have given to him. Let us all look to You for salvation in this time and also in the future. In the name of Jesus our Savior, we pray. Amen.

One third of the earth was burned up, and one third of the trees were burned up, and all green grass was burned up. This is exceedingly bad. One third of the grass includes all grain crops: rice, corn, and barley. One third of trees includes fruit and nut trees. The only way mankind can survive is to turn to God.

April 21 – Revelation 8:8-9

The second angel sounded, and something like a great burning mountain was thrown into the sea. One third of the sea became blood,[9] and one third of the living creatures which were in the sea died. One third of the ships were destroyed.

What happened at the second trumpet?

1.

2.

What were the effects of the second trumpet?

1.

2.

What would be the effects on mankind?

Prayer: Holy Father, help us to be worthy to escape these disasters and punishments to come on all the world. Let our eyes always be fixed on You for deliverance through Jesus Christ, and not through the strength of man. In Jesus's Name, we pray. Amen.

One third of the ships were destroyed. This sentence is last, but it may have the biggest impact on mankind. One third of ships means all world commerce declines by one third. All exports and imports decline by one third. Likely the impact on the world's economy will be greater than a one-third decline. This will be an immediate worldwide depression.

April 22 – Revelation 8:10-11

The third angel sounded, and a great star fell from the sky, burning like a torch, and it fell on one third of the rivers, and on the springs of the waters.[11] The name of the star is called "Wormwood." One third of the waters became wormwood. Many people died from the waters, because they were made bitter.

What happened at the third trumpet?

1.

2.

3.

What were the effects of the third trumpet?

1.

2.

3.

What would be the effects on mankind?

Prayer: Father, we look to You as our source of living water in Jesus Christ. Let us not drink of the bitter poison of the world, but only from Your sweet Source. In the Name of the Way, the Truth, and the Life we pray. Amen.

The name of the star is called "Wormwood." Wormwood is an herb used in liquors and medicines. It's known for its bitterness, and it is fatal in large doses. This does not mean the meteor described is literal wormwood, just similar in its effects.

April 23 – Revelation 8:12

The fourth angel sounded, and one third of the sun was struck, and one third of the moon, and one third of the stars; so that one third of them would be darkened, and the day wouldn't shine for one third of it, and the night in the same way.

What happened at the fourth trumpet?

1.

2.

3.

What were the effects of the fourth trumpet?

1.

2.

What would be the effects on mankind?

Prayer: Holy God, You are our Light and salvation in dark times. You strike at the light You gave mankind, for mankind has struck at Your Light, Jesus Christ. Let us not despair in dark times, but instead look to You at all times. In Jesus's Name, we pray. Amen.

The day wouldn't shine for one third of it, and the night in the same way. From this description, it appears one third of the Earth's sky is completely blacked out. How could God do this? A black cloud of material between the Earth and the Sun or between the Earth and the Moon could achieve this result. The answer is up to God.

April 24 – Revelation 8:13

I saw, and I heard an angel, flying in mid heaven, saying with a loud voice, "Woe! Woe! Woe for those who dwell on the earth, because of the other voices of the trumpets of the three angels, who are yet to sound!"

Who warns mankind?

What is the warning?

How many woes are mentioned?

How many trumpets remain?

Prayer: Father, You warned Adam and Eve their choice of sin would lead to suffering and woe, and so we've seen it throughout history. Now when all the sin of mankind comes to a head, we cry to You for deliverance from Your righteous judgments. Save us, O Lord Jesus Christ! Amen.

"Because of the other voices of the trumpets of the three angels, who are yet to sound!" As horrible as the first four trumpets have been, the next three are to surpass them, so much so that God sends an angel to warn mankind. "Mid heaven" would be in the atmosphere, where all humanity can hear the warning. Why would God bother? Because He still seeks to save as many as possible during these plagues.

April 25 – Revelation 9:1

The fifth angel sounded, and I saw a star from the sky which had fallen to the earth. The key to the pit of the abyss was given to him.

Who receives this key to the abyss?

How can a star be a person and receive a key?

Why was this key given to this person?

Prayer: Father, You are sovereign over all, and You determine who may rule and who may be taken from rulership. Even Satan comes and goes at Your command. Help us to accept and endure even the worst rulers, knowing that You, Jesus Christ, are over all, using them to work Your purposes. Increase our faith, Lord! Amen.

And I saw a star from the sky which had fallen to the earth. Jesus Christ Himself addresses this event:

Luke 10:17-18 *The seventy returned with joy, saying, "Lord, even the demons are subject to us in your name!"*[18] *He said to them, "I saw Satan having fallen like lightning from heaven."*

Thus Jesus identifies this "star" as Satan. God, in His address to Job, speaks of angels as stars:

Job 38:6-7 *What were its foundations fastened on? Or who laid its cornerstone,*[7] *when the morning stars sang together, and all the sons of God shouted for joy?*

April 26 – Revelation 9:2

He opened the pit of the abyss, and smoke went up out of the pit, like the smoke from a burning furnace. The sun and the air were darkened because of the smoke from the pit.

What is done with the key?

What comes out of the pit?

What is the effect on the Earth?

Prayer: Father, You instructed us to dress and keep the garden, which includes the whole Earth. We have failed and have besmirched Your creation. It is no wonder You allow us to suffer the consequences of polluting heaven, Earth, and seas. Forgive us, and teach us to live with love toward You, our fellow man, and the Earth You've created. In Jesus's Name, we pray. Amen.

Like the smoke from a burning furnace. Furnaces have been around for thousands of years for smelting metals and burning bricks. The vivid image of air pollution from these furnaces reflects Satan's first action at opening the abyss.

April 27 – Revelation 9:3

And there came out of the smoke locusts upon the earth: and unto them was given power, as the scorpions of the earth have power.

What comes out of the smoke?

What power do the locusts have?

What power do scorpions have?

Prayer: Dear God, one dreadful image follows another. Who would not fear a plague of locusts ruining the countryside? And then these locusts have stings like scorpions. Father, please save us from such things through our Savior Jesus Christ. In His Name, Amen.

And there came out of the smoke locusts upon the earth. A plague of locusts is a common curse in the Bible. It happened to Egypt as one of the ten plagues, and then later it happened to Israel in the book of Joel. The insects strip the country bare of green things. Yet these are not literal locusts, for they have stings like scorpions. We find out more about them in the rest of **Revelation 9.**

April 28 – Revelation 9:4

They were told that they should not hurt the grass of the earth, neither any green thing, neither any tree, but only those people who don't have God's seal on their foreheads.

What are the locusts commanded?

1.

2.

3.

4.

Who are those who don't have God's seal on their foreheads?

Prayer: Father, we pray for Your seal of approval, through Jesus Christ our Lord, in the Holy Spirit of truth. Let us firmly embrace You and Your will through all trials and troubles, we pray. Amen.

Only those people who don't have God's seal on their foreheads. We covered the sealing of God's people in chapter 7. This locust army of Satan was not permitted to harm them, but only those who are not God's followers.

April 29 – Revelation 9:5

They were given power, not to kill them, but to torment them for five months. Their torment was like the torment of a scorpion when it strikes a person.

What was the torment like?

How long does this torment last?

Prayer: O Father, swiftly bring an end to this time of suffering. We know You are working out Your purposes here on the Earth, but our hearts move with compassion for those who suffer so. In Jesus's Name, we pray. Amen.

Like the torment of a scorpion when it strikes a person. A quick online search revealed these symptoms: numbness all over your body, difficulty breathing, difficulty swallowing, slurred speech, restlessness, seizures, roving eye movements, muscle twitching, irregular heartbeat, and abdominal pain. The next few verses will reveal more about these locusts/scorpions.

April 30 – Revelation 9:6

In those days people will seek death, and will in no way find it. They will desire to die, and death will flee from them.

How do people react to the locust/scorpion army?

Why will they be unable to escape from the locust/scorpion army?

Prayer: You are our God of life and hope. Without hope, people do not desire life. Give hope to all mankind, Jesus Christ, so all will seek You, the Way, the Truth, and the Life. Amen.

People will seek death, and will in no way find it. We can only speculate on what prevents this desire for mass suicide. One explanation is that a worldwide dictatorship prevents any suicide effort. Another explanation is that the victims are unable to move and commit suicide. Regardless, this is a horrible time for all mankind.

May 1 – Revelation 9:7

The shapes of the locusts were like horses prepared for war. On their heads were something like golden crowns, and their faces were like people's faces.

What was the shape of the locust beings?

What was on the heads?

What were their faces like?

Prayer: Father, let us pray now to be accounted worthy to escape these coming plagues. If we enter such trials, grant us courage and strength to remain faithful to You. In the Name of our all-sufficient Redeemer, Jesus Christ, we pray. Amen.

Their faces were like people's faces. This vivid description has given rise to a great deal of speculation about the nature of these locusts. Some have thought of literal horsemen, and some have thought of helicopters, or some other kind of military aircraft. God can hide the nature of these future events and yet give us enough detail so that when they happen we say, "Oh, that is it. I recognize what this is from prophecy."

May 2 - Revelation 9:8

They had hair like women's hair, and their teeth were like those of lions.

What do the locusts look like?

1.

2.

What do you think is literal and what do you think is figurative?

Prayer: Father in heaven, help us wait patiently and humbly for the fulfillment of Your word. We love having glimpses into the future and want to know exactly what will happen. But You hide things from everyone in plain sight, such as the first coming of Jesus Christ and the salvation of all mankind. How much more are smaller details hidden? Help us be humble and patient. In Jesus's Name, we pray. Amen.

They had hair like women's hair. Is this literal or figurative? Are these actual women or actual men with long hair? Or is this a machine or a monster with long hair-like attachments to its head? We simply don't know. This is the future. We must wait for the fulfillment to see what it is. To admit we don't know is very freeing.

May 3 - Revelation 9:9

They had breastplates, like breastplates of iron. The sound of their wings was like the sound of chariots, or of many horses rushing to war.

What are their breastplates like?

What do their wings sound like?

What do you think is the best explanation for the locust-like horsemen?

Prayer: Thank You, Father, for stimulating our imaginations and our minds with these vivid, and yet cryptic, descriptions of the future. Dwelling on Your Word will lead us to a greater understanding of You and ourselves. Help us to persist in our study! In the Name of the Word of God, we pray. Amen.

The sound of their wings was like the sound of chariots, or of many horses rushing to war. We're not too familiar with the sound of chariots, that of many wooden or metal wheels on the hard ground. Perhaps the closest is in old Western movies that show runaway wagons or stagecoaches. We're more familiar with the sound of a herd or troop of horses galloping. In both cases, the rumbling sound would mean death to a town or soldiers awaiting the charge of brutal death.

May 4 – Revelation 9:10

They have tails like those of scorpions, and stings. In their tails they have power to harm men for five months.

How do the tail and sting of a scorpion operate?

How would you feel anticipating a painful sting, based upon the noise of the locusts?

How would you feel between and after the attacks?

Prayer: Father, there is much to fear in this world—pain, death, disease, injury, disasters, or the wars of men. Yet You promise us peace and freedom from fear in Jesus Christ, our Prince of Peace. We claim this promise now in His Name. Amen.

They have tails like those of scorpions, and stings. Flying scorpions would certainly qualify as the subject of a monster or horror movie. Multiplying their numbers into a swarm of locusts makes it worse. These may be human-directed machines of war, which adds intelligence and malice to the equation. This is truly the worst trumpet plague so far.

May 5 – Revelation 9:11

They have over them as king the angel of the abyss. His name in Hebrew is "Abaddon[3]," but in Greek, he has the name "Apollyon[4]"

Who is the king over the locusts?

Who else is called a destroyer in the Bible?

Who else is called a murderer in the New Testament?

Prayer: Father, save us from the destroyer, whomever he may be. Deliver us through the blood of Jesus, as You saved the children of Israel from the destroying angel in Egypt. In Jesus's Name, we pray. Amen.

His name in Hebrew is "Abaddon,"– A search of the Bible for the word "destroyer" includes the death angel in **Exodus 12:23**, Samson in **Judges 16:24**, and Babylon in **Isaiah 16:4**. **Jeremiah 51:48-56** also calls Persia Babylon's destroyer. In general, we see that a "destroyer" kills people and may be angelic, a person, or a nation.

May 6 – Revelation 9:12

The first woe is past. Behold, there are still two woes coming after this.

What was the first woe?

What are the next two woes?

Will they be as bad as the first woe, better, or worse? Why do you think so?

Prayer: Your justice flows inexorably, Lord God Almighty. When people sin, woes come. When the whole world sins, woes come upon the whole world. Yet with Your judgments, You have mercy, saving those who repent through Jesus Christ. Help us repent now, Lord, and be spared from woes now and later. Amen.

Behold, there are still two woes coming after this. The first woe was the fifth trumpet. Logically, the sixth and seventh trumpets will be the next two woes. How can they be worse than what has already happened?

May 7 – Revelation 9:13-14

The sixth angel sounded. I heard a voice from the horns of the golden altar which is before God,[14] saying to the sixth angel who had the trumpet, "Free the four angels who are bound at the great river Euphrates!"

What is the source of the voice from the horns of the golden altar?

Where previously has the golden altar been mentioned in Revelation?

What was happening when this altar was mentioned?

Prayer – Father, Revelation shows You using angels for many purposes, without naming them or giving them recognition. Yet they are obedient to Your commands, executing them faithfully. Help us to faithfully perform Your commands to us here on Earth, no matter how difficult they may seem, even if we receive no recognition. In Jesus's Name, we pray. Amen.

"Free the four angels who are bound at the great river Euphrates!" This statement causes more questions to arise: Why were the angels bound? When were they bound? What will they do next? So it is with the whole book of Revelation. Yet we learn angels can be bound and limited to certain geographic locations. This fact alone explains some angelic statements in **Daniel 10**.

May 8 – Revelation 9:15

The four angels were freed who had been prepared for that hour and day and month and year, so that they might kill one third of mankind.

How long were the angels prepared for their task?

What was their task?

Do you think these are good or evil angels?

Prayer: Father, before Jesus's return a worse time than the flood will hit the Earth. Help us to endure this time and to be counted worthy to escape all these things. In Jesus's Name, we pray. Amen

So that they might kill one third of mankind. Here is the answer for what might be worse than the first five trumpets — the deaths of a third of mankind. As I write this, we're past eight billion in population worldwide, so this number would be close to three billion. We do not know when this will happen or how many might be alive. In any case, it will be horrible.

May 9 – Revelation 9:16

The number of the armies of the horsemen was two hundred million. I heard the number of them.

What is the sixth trumpet and second woe?

What else appears with this woe?

Who can field an army of this size?

Prayer: Father, the world survived World Wars I and II, with the deaths of over one hundred million people. Without Jesus, the world would not survive this war. Come soon, Lord Jesus, Prince of Peace, and bring peace to this world! Amen.

The number of the armies of the horsemen was two hundred million. This is the largest army the world has ever known. This is the result of thousands of years of increasing war technology combined with an increasing population. Sadly, the human heart is still bent on war.

May 10 – Revelation 9:17

Thus I saw the horses in the vision, and those who sat on them, having breastplates of fiery red, hyacinth blue, and sulfur yellow; and the horses' heads resembled lions' heads. Out of their mouths proceed fire, smoke, and sulfur.

What were the horsemen like?

1.

2.

What were the horses like?

1.

2.

Do you think these are literal horses?

Do you think these are literal horsemen?

Prayer: Father, we are limited in what we know and what we can imagine. You appointed John to write what he saw. Let us learn what lessons we can, with only our limited understanding of what will happen in the future. In Jesus's Name, we pray. Amen.

And those who sat on them, having breastplates… John was familiar with horses, horsemen, and breastplates. These he'd seen all his life in the Roman Empire. We can only imagine what he saw in his vision: some kind of humans in armor, on some kind of transportation with a "mouth" out of which came fire, smoke, and sulfur. These are the three things that come out of a gun or cannon.

May 11 - Revelation 9:18

By these three plagues were one third of mankind killed: by the fire, the smoke, and the sulfur, which proceeded out of their mouths.

How did the horses kill one third of mankind?

1.

2.

3.

What do you think is literal and what is figurative?

Prayer: Our Father in heaven, You know how everything will turn out, and You led John to use these words in the book of Revelation You gave to Jesus. Help us to wait patiently on You through the worst trials that may happen to us and to never give up our sure hope in Jesus Christ. In His Name, we pray. Amen.

One third of mankind was killed: by the fire, the smoke, and the sulfur. One interpretation is this is simply a modern gun or cannon. This is precisely what comes out of the barrel. Or it could be three modes of death: flame, suffocation, and poisoning by deadly gas or powder. We don't know for sure. But we are warned.

May 12 - Revelation 9:19

For the power of the horses is in their mouths and in their tails. For their tails are like serpents, and have heads, and with them they harm.

Where is the power of the horses?

1.

2.

How does the power of the tails of the horses differ from that of the mouth?

1.

2.

Prayer: Father, through Jesus we face torture and death, just as He did for us. Help us to live without fear, knowing and claiming your promise that You will allow no trial that is too hard for us, but with the trial, You will provide a way of escape. In His Name, we claim this promise. Amen. (See **1 Corinthians 10:13.**)

Their tails are like serpents, and have heads, and with them they harm. This chimera-like feature seems to be like a poisonous serpent. Those who would attack this "cavalry" from the rear (a normal military tactic, especially with armored vehicles) will be harmed by this rear-facing tail. What is it? We don't know. It seems to cause harm but not death. Perhaps a sonic weapon of some kind? Tear gas? Poison gas?

May 13 – Revelation 9:20-21

The rest of mankind, who were not killed with these plagues, didn't repent of the works of their hands, that they wouldn't worship demons, and the idols of gold, and of silver, and of brass, and of stone, and of wood; which can't see, hear, or walk.[21] They didn't repent of their murders, their sorceries, their sexual immorality, or their thefts.

How did two-thirds of mankind react to the death of one-third of humanity?

What were the works of mankind?

1.

2.

3.

4.

5.

6.

Prayer: Father, over and over You instruct us to flee idolatry. Nonetheless, we see more and more idols around us as people serve and worship money, possessions, careers, political parties, and other people. Let us not be caught up with the frenzy of materialism and idol worship of our culture, but instead focus on You and Your Word as we grow in Jesus. Amen.

The rest of mankind ... didn't repent of the works of their hands. Very often when people narrowly escape death they turn to God in gratitude. This isn't a consideration for anyone in the world. Rather, the entire world continues on a "business as usual" basis. There isn't even mention of grieving or sadness for those who were killed. This tells us much about society at this time.

May 14 - Revelation 10:1

I saw a mighty angel coming down out of the sky, clothed with a cloud. A rainbow was on his head. His face was like the sun, and his feet like pillars of fire.

Where did the angel come from?

How did the mighty angel appear?

Was this angel visible to all the Earth or just to John in the vision?

Prayer: Who can stand before one of Your mighty servants, let alone You, Almighty God? You array Your angels gloriously, and they cause awe in those who see them. Help us to heed You, Who sits enthroned above all. In Jesus's Name, we pray. Amen.

I saw a mighty angel coming down out of the sky, clothed with a cloud. This is part of John's vision that appears to be on the Earth. Remember, John's point of view is from heaven, before God's throne, as established in **Revelation 4** and **5**. Through the seals and trumpets, John has a clear view of what is happening on Earth. It is helpful to remember John's perspective as we ask and seek the answers to our questions.

May 15 – Revelation 10:2

He had in his hand a little open book. He set his right foot on the sea, and his left on the land.

What did the angel hold in his hand?

Where did the angel stand?

How did the angel stand?

Prayer: You give us pictures and stories to teach us, holy Father. Let us listen carefully and understand what You say and respond so we may please You. In Jesus's Name, we pray. Amen.

He set his right foot on the sea, and his left on the land. This vision is like a parable that interrupts the narrative flow of trumpets in **Revelation 8 and 9**. In a parable, each element has a meaning. The angel is a messenger from God. The book has a meaning that's covered later. The stance is on Earth, with one foot on land and one on the sea, suggesting the message encompasses both or is for the inhabitants of both.

May 16 – Revelation 10:3

He cried with a loud voice, as a lion roars. When he cried, the seven thunders uttered their voices.

How did the angel speak?

What happened when the angel spoke?

Prayer: Father, You picture this message to us, but You cloak the meaning. Help us to obey You even when we don't understand what You say or what is happening. In the Name of the Son, we pray. Amen.

He cried with a loud voice, as a lion roars. Lions command our attention with their roars. They intimidate their prey and cause them to flee. In this way Your angel communicates, with the authority of the Lion of the tribe of Judah.

May 17 – Revelation 10:4

When the seven thunders sounded, I was about to write; but I heard a voice from the sky saying, "Seal up the things which the seven thunders said, and don't write them."

What was John's instruction about the seven thunders?

Were these thunders heard on Earth?

Who understood the seven thunders?

Prayer: Father, in Revelation You shift our perspective from heaven to Earth and back again. Help us accept that we will not understand some things until the proper time, when You will reveal them. Thank You for Your revelation! Amen.

When the seven thunders sounded, I was about to write. Back in **Revelation 1:10**, John's instruction was, *"What you see, write in a book and send to the seven assemblies [which are in Asia]: to Ephesus, Smyrna, Pergamum, Thyatira, Sardis, Philadelphia, and to Laodicea."* John also included what he heard in his vision. But in this case, God forbade him from recording it.

May 18 – Revelation 10:5-7

The angel whom I saw standing on the sea and on the land lifted up his right hand to the sky,[6] and swore by him who lives forever and ever, who created heaven and the things that are in it, the earth and the things that are in it, and the sea and the things that are in it, that there will no longer be delay,[7] but in the days of the voice of the seventh angel, when he is about to sound, then the mystery of God is finished, as he declared to his servants, the prophets.

To Whom did the angel swear?

What did the angel swear?

What will be finished?

Who knows about the mystery of God?

Prayer: Father, thank You that You have revealed Your mysteries to us, Your people, through Your prophets. Thank You for giving us what understanding we have. We have but a little, but it is enough. In Jesus's Name, we pray. Amen.

There will no longer be delay,[7] but in the days of the voice of the seventh angel … then the mystery of God is finished. In case we didn't have enough anticipation about the seventh trumpet to come and finish the third woe and the cycle of trumpets, God highlights it. God, through His angel, declares all His mystery, as He declared to all His prophets, is completed in the days of the seventh trumpet. This takes my breath away. There are hundreds of prophecies about the "day of the Lord" and the "end times."

May 19 – Revelation 10:8

The voice which I heard from heaven, again speaking with me, said, "Go, take the book which is open in the hand of the angel who stands on the sea and on the land."

What was John commanded by the voice from heaven?

What type of book was this?

Where was this book?

Where was John?

Prayer: Father, thank You for involving us in Your great acts throughout history. You have us play parts that You have trained us to perform. When our opportunity comes, help us, like John, to be ready to take Your book and do Your will. in Jesus's Name, we pray. Amen.

"Go, take the book which is open in the hand of the angel." This is likely a scroll, perhaps the same as the one Jesus unsealed, perhaps a different one. John acts out his part by taking the message from God and speaking it to the world. We should do the same.

May 20 – Revelation 10:9

I went to the angel, telling him to give me the little book. He said to me, "Take it, and eat it. It will make your stomach bitter, but in your mouth it will be as sweet as honey."

What was John commanded by the angel?

What does the angel tell him about the book?

1.

2.

Prayer: Father, very often we love to hear Your words of beauty and love. We delight that You love us and forgive all our sins. But then when we understand Your Word and try living by it, we find it bitter to obey, to love and forgive our enemies, even those who grievously hurt us. Help us to digest Your Word and live it! In the Name of the Word of God, we pray. Amen.

Take it, and eat it. Eating a scroll is a startling, even bizarre, image. Yet it is a familiar one to John, who knew Ezekiel had done the same thing. Ezekiel ate a scroll from God in a vision and then spoke it to Israel.

Ezekiel 3:1-4 *He said to me, "Son of man, eat what you find. Eat this scroll, and go, speak to the house of Israel."² So I opened my mouth, and he caused me to eat the scroll.³ He said to me, "Son of man, cause your belly to eat, and fill your bowels with this scroll that I give you." Then I ate it; and it was as sweet as honey in my mouth.⁴ He said to me, "Son of man, go to the house of Israel, and speak my words to them."*

May 21 – Revelation 10:10

I took the little book out of the angel's hand, and ate it. It was as sweet as honey in my mouth. When I had eaten it, my stomach was made bitter.

What did John do?

What happened to John?

What does this tell us about the word of God?

Prayer: Father, very often You warn us of disastrous consequences of sin and sometimes of evil that will come for doing good. Let us never doubt that the least word of Yours will truly come to pass. Increase our faith, Lord. Amen.

I took the little book out of the angel's hand and ate it. Notice the exact correspondence with Ezekiel's experience. This passage comes directly before the previous one you read yesterday:

Ezekiel 2:8-10 *"Open your mouth, and eat that which I give you."*[9] *When I looked, behold, a hand was stretched out to me; and, behold, a scroll of a book was in it.*[10] *He spread it before me. It was written within and without; and lamentations, mourning, and woe were written in it.*

We eat one bite at a time. So we should read God's Word, understanding it, one piece at a time.

May 22 – Revelation 10:11

He told me, "You must prophesy again over many peoples, nations, languages, and kings."

What was the second command from the angel to John?

To whom was John sent?

1.

2.

3.

4.

How does this differ from Ezekiel's instruction from yesterday?

Prayer: Jesus, before You ascended to heaven You instructed us to "Go you therefore into all the world and preach the gospel to everyone." We've been trying to do this for thousands of years. It is encouraging You've preserved the book of Revelation for us and for the world, to give the good news in very bleak times. Help us to speak it to all! Amen.

"**You must prophesy again over many peoples, nations, languages, and kings.**" "Prophesy" is simply speaking God's word. "Peoples" are of different kinds, regardless of where they live. "Nations" is "*ethnos*" in Greek—ethnicities, who live in various geographic regions with a common government and culture. "Languages" can separate us, but we must overcome this to obey Christ. "Kings" are rulers of governments, whether mayors, governors, presidents, dictators, premiers, or literal kings. This is a huge assignment for the church, but with Jesus's help, it will be done.

May 23 - Revelation 11:1

A reed like a rod was given to me. Someone said, "Rise, and measure God's temple, and the altar, and those who worship in it."

What was the third command from the angel to John?

What was John to measure?

1.

2.

3.

What is the temple?

What is the altar?

Who worships there?

Prayer: O Lord God Almighty, help us understand Your words and measure up to the standard of Jesus Christ, our King and our Lord. Amen.

"Measure God's temple, and the altar, and those who worship in it." God's temple was a specific building until the Church started on Pentecost. Since then it has been the Church where God dwells. The altar may refer to the sacrificial altar outside the temple or the altar of incense inside the temple. Revelation has already mentioned the altar of incense, where the prayers of the saints come before God. Jesus Christ's sacrifice replaced all animal sacrifices, tearing away the veil and allowing all people to come to Him. The final measurement is on the worshippers in the Church.

May 24 - Revelation 11:2

Leave out the court which is outside of the temple, and don't measure it, for it has been given to the nations. They will tread the holy city under foot for forty-two months.

What was the fourth command given to John by the angel?

What is the court outside the temple?

To whom is it given?

What will the nations do to the holy city?

Prayer: O Father, the time is fleeting. Help as many as possible to move from outside the temple, the Church, to inside, so they will not be outside during the end-time events. In the Name of our soon-coming Jesus, we pray. Amen.

Leave out the court which is outside of the temple. The physical temple had a large court outside where people could gather and enter the inner court. So the Church has the whole world outside of it, where people may enter if they wish. It is given to all the world's nations, all ethnicities.

May 25 – Revelation 11:3

I will give power to my two witnesses, and they will prophesy one thousand two hundred sixty days, clothed in sackcloth."

What are the two witnesses given?

What shall they do?

How long shall they prophesy?

How shall they prophesy?

Prayer: Father, help us remember that we, too, are Your witnesses, and You have instructed us to testify to Jesus Christ in our words and deeds. If we are inarticulate, help our deeds of love speak clearly of Christ. Give us His power as You promised. In Jesus's Name, we pray. Amen.

They will prophesy one thousand two hundred sixty days, clothed in sackcloth. Sackcloth indicates mourning and humility, an attitude of seeking God. The end-time events will stir these two with the Spirit of God to accomplish God's prophetic purpose. Twelve hundred and sixty days is the same as forty-two months or three-and-a-half years. Their ministry appears to coincide with the end times with the seals and trumpets.

May 26 – Revelation 11:4

These are the two olive trees and the two lamp stands, standing before the Lord of the earth.

What are the two witnesses called?

1.

2.

Before Whom do they stand?

Prayer: Almighty God, You use one symbol after another in the book of Revelation. Help us not to be overwhelmed but to carefully research each symbol within the book and its meaning elsewhere in the Bible. In the Name of the Word of God, we pray. Amen.

These are the two olive trees and the two lamp stands. This image comes from an Old Testament prophet:

Zechariah 4:2-3 *I said, "I have seen, and behold, a lampstand all of gold, with its bowl on the top of it, and its seven lamps on it; there are seven pipes to each of the lamps, which are on the top of it;[3] and two olive trees by it, one on the right side of the bowl, and the other on the left side of it."*

Zechariah himself didn't know the meaning of the vision, but the angel explained it:

Zechariah 4:12, 14 *I asked him … "What are these two olive branches, which are beside the two golden spouts, that pour the golden oil out of themselves?"[14] Then he said, "These are the two anointed ones who stand by the Lord of the whole earth."*

May 27 – Revelation 11:5

If anyone desires to harm them, fire proceeds out of their mouth and devours their enemies. If anyone desires to harm them, he must be killed in this way.

What can the two witnesses do to those who would hurt them?

Why would anyone desire to hurt them?

How would the world react to these witnesses?

Prayer: Father, the weakest and most vulnerable members of society, when they seek Your protection, are protected indeed. These humble prophets, teaching people about God, are opposed, and people try to kill them. You return their deeds upon their heads. You are just, O God! Amen.

Fire proceeds out of their mouth and devours their enemies. This extraordinary statement and power have an Old Testament precedent:

2 Kings 1:9-10 *Then the king sent a captain of fifty with his fifty to him. He went up to him; and behold, he was sitting on the top of the hill. He said to him, "Man of God, the king has said, 'Come down!'"* [10] *Elijah answered to the captain of fifty, "If I am a man of God, then let fire come down from the sky, and consume you and your fifty!" Then fire came down from the sky, and consumed him and his fifty.*

So these two witnesses will have similar power to that of Elijah.

May 28 – Revelation 11:6

These have the power to shut up the sky, that it may not rain during the days of their prophecy. They have power over the waters, to turn them into blood, and to strike the earth with every plague, as often as they desire.

What other miraculous powers do these two witnesses have?

1.

2.

3.

Prayer: Holy Father, we can't imagine having that sort of power—yet it is Yours to give. Whatever power and authority You do give us, help us to use it wisely, according to Your will. In Jesus's Name, we pray. Amen.

They have power over the waters, to turn them into blood. The first two powers, calling down fire from heaven and causing drought, are powers Elijah used. The next two powers, turning water into blood and other plagues, are powers Moses used. Some think these two witnesses will be Moses and Elijah resurrected. But no one knows for sure.

May 29 – Revelation 11:7

When they have finished their testimony, the beast that comes up out of the abyss will make war with them, and overcome them, and kill them.

What happens to the two witnesses after their testimony?

Who kills them?

Prayer: Holy God Almighty, You have done many miracles in our lives, from our birth to our salvation until now. Help us to give our testimony faithfully to all without fear, even of fear of death, for You have conquered death. In the Name of the Way, the Truth, and the Life, Amen.

The beast that comes up out of the abyss will make war with them. Who is this beast? First, the fallen angel opens the pit, and then the locust army comes out. This beast seems to be the same as the locust army or is the leader of that army.

May 30 – Revelation 11:8

Their dead bodies will be in the street of the great city, which spiritually is called Sodom and Egypt, where also their Lord was crucified.

What happens to their bodies?

Which city is this?

Prayer – Ah Lord God, we love You, but we fear death. Help us to love You enough to die for You, just as Jesus loves us and died for us. Let us look to our lives past death. In the Savior's Name, we pray. Amen.

Which spiritually is called Sodom and Egypt, where also their Lord was crucified - God's prophets often used Sodom and Gomorrah as warnings for sinful cities and peoples: **Isaiah 13:19** – Chaldea (Babylon); **Jeremiah 23:14** – Jerusalem; **Jeremiah 49:18** – Samaria; **Jeremiah 50:40** – Babylon; **Amos 4:11** – Israel; **Zephaniah 2:9** – Moab. However, only Jerusalem is where Jesus was crucified.

This fact identifies where the two witnesses preached and were killed.

May 31 – Revelation 11:9

From among the peoples, tribes, languages, and nations, people will look at their dead bodies for three and a half days, and will not allow their dead bodies to be laid in a tomb.

Who will cause their bodies to be not buried?

How long will their bodies lie there?

Prayer: O Lord Jesus, You were hated and killed, by both Your people and those of Rome, unjustly and cruelly. Yet You forgave Your killers, and us, Your people whom You have saved. Help us also forgive those who persecute us for following You and teaching Your words. In Your Name, we pray. Amen.

From among the peoples, tribes, languages, and nations, people will look at their dead bodies. We've seen this phrase before in **Revelation 10:11**. This is the whole world.

June 1 – Revelation 11:10

Those who dwell on the earth rejoice over them, and they will be glad. They will give gifts to one another because these two prophets tormented those who dwell on the earth.

What else will the world do?

Why will the world rejoice at their deaths?

How were they tormented by the witnesses?

Prayer: Father, the world, led by Satan, calls evil good and good evil. Thus they kill Your prophets and rejoice over their deaths. Let us never cling to this world but to You and Jesus Christ, our Savior and Lord. In His Name, we pray. Amen.

Because these two prophets tormented those who dwell on the earth. How can Christians torment non-Christians? First, by teaching them their deeds are evil. Everyone wants to be good, and no one wants to be called evil. Second, by acknowledging God is Ruler over all. Not human government, nor human religion, not even our own will has authority over God. It is considered narrow-minded to claim Jesus is the only Way, the only Truth, and the only way to life.

June 2 – Revelation 11:11

And after three days and a half the Spirit of life from God entered into them, and they stood upon their feet.

What happens to their bodies after three-and-a-half days?

How do you think the world reacts to their resurrection?

Prayer: Father, You and Jesus Christ are our hope beyond this life, beyond death, beyond the grave. In You alone is eternal life. Help us to keep our eyes fixed on Jesus, our Salvation. In the Name of the Resurrection, we pray. Amen.

The Spirit of life from God entered into them. This phrase is like that in Ezekiel:

Ezekiel 37:14 *"I will put my Spirit in you, and you will live. Then I will place you in your own land; and you will know that I, Yahweh, have spoken it and performed it," says Yahweh.*

This is from the resurrection of the valley of dry bones that Ezekiel saw in his vision.

June 3 – Revelation 11:12

I heard a loud voice from heaven saying to them, "Come up here!" They went up into heaven in the cloud, and their enemies saw them.

What happens after their resurrection?

Who sees them ascend to heaven in a cloud?

Prayer: O Holy Father, Your enemies never triumph, but You always do. Where humanly we see death as an end and a defeat, for You it is the start of the greater victory You have planned from the beginning. We praise You for Your victory over death, in the Name of the One Who conquered death. Amen.

They went up into heaven in the cloud, and their enemies saw them. This is like the people resurrected at Jesus's resurrection.

Matthew 27:52-53 *The tombs were opened, and many bodies of the saints who had fallen asleep were raised;[53] and coming out of the tombs after his resurrection, they entered into the holy city and appeared to many.*

Also, like Jesus, these witnesses ascended to heaven visibly.

Acts 1:9 *When He had said these things, as they were looking, He was taken up, and a cloud received Him out of their sight.*

June 4 – Revelation 11:13

In that day there was a great earthquake, and a tenth of the city fell. Seven thousand people were killed in the earthquake, and the rest were terrified, and gave glory to the God of heaven

What else happens at the two witnesses' resurrection?

1.

2.

3.

4.

Prayer: Father, You are indomitable. When Satan does everything to thwart Your plan of salvation, You use Satan's every effort to further Your plan. You even take the martyrdom of Your two witnesses and use that to save the citizens of Jerusalem. Glory to You forever! Amen.

The rest were terrified, and gave glory to the God of heaven. Notice the order of events: 1. An earthquake destroys a tenth of Jerusalem and kills seven thousand people. 2. The rest of the city was frightened. They had narrowly escaped death. 3. The living glorified God. Was this a conversion? I believe so, for the two witnesses had preached the gospel for three and a half years. They knew the God of heaven.

June 5 – Revelation 11:14-15

The second woe is past. Behold, the third woe comes quickly.[15] The seventh angel sounded, and great voices in heaven followed, saying, "The kingdom of the world has become the Kingdom of our Lord, and of his Christ. He will reign forever and ever!"

When is the seventh trumpet and third woe?

What is said by voices in heaven at the seventh trumpet?

How does the world change at the seventh trumpet?

Prayer: O Father, from the time Adam and Eve sinned and You promised the woman a seed who would crush the serpent's head, we've been waiting for the end of Satan's world rule. Now here Jesus Christ takes His throne. Let us press forward toward this day bravely and relentlessly. In the Name of the King, Amen.

The kingdom of the world has become the Kingdom of our Lord, and of his Christ. "Under new management" is a sign of hope and change. The new King will be different from the lies, corruption, and destruction of Satan. Instead, we can expect truth, justice for all. and a worldwide building program. The whole Earth will become a garden of Eden—and better.

June 6 – Revelation 11:16

The twenty-four elders, who sit on their thrones before God's throne, fell on their faces and worshiped God,

What do the twenty-four elders do at the seventh trumpet?

Why do they do this at the seventh trumpet?

Prayer: Father in heaven, we, too, worship You and Jesus Christ. You carried out Your plan to give mankind eternal life and rulership over the world, despite Satan seeking to wreck it. You, Jesus Christ, bore the penalty for our many sins, and You Yourself will be our perfect King and Ruler. We worship You! Amen.

The twenty-four elders, who sit on their thrones before God's throne. Imagine the perspective of these heavenly beings in God's Presence for billions of years. They have seen the universe and the Earth formed, the ages of life on the Earth until man was created. They saw Satan's rebellion and man's sin, and all hope seemed lost. Now they see the culmination of God's plan and must worship.

June 7 – Revelation 11:17

Saying: "We give you thanks, Lord God, the Almighty, the one who is and who was, and who is coming, because You have taken Your great power and reigned."

What do the twenty-four elders say?

What is their first reaction to God Almighty taking the rule of the Earth?

Why do they have this reaction?

Prayer: Father, it's hard to believe, but we can help You rule the Earth—if we let You rule our lives. Help us to surrender to You and Your government in our lives, following Jesus Christ as our King and our God. In His Name, we pray. Amen.

"Because You have taken Your great power and reigned." The issue has never been Satan's power against God's power. God can take His power and rule the Earth at any time. Rather, God's whole focus is on saving as many people as possible, even during Satan's rule.

2 Peter 3:9 *The Lord is not slow concerning his promise, as some count slowness; but he is patient with us, not wishing that anyone should perish, but that all should come to repentance.*

June 8 – Revelation 11:18

"The nations were angry, and your wrath came, as did the time for the dead to be judged, and to give your bondservants the prophets, their reward, as well as to the saints, and those who fear your name, to the small and the great, and to destroy those who destroy the earth."

What else do the twenty-four elders say?

1.

2.

3.

4.

5.

Prayer: Father in heaven, we are comforted that You have given all judgment to Jesus Christ, Who died to save us. Not only does He spare our lives with His very blood, but He also works as our Advocate, defending us from Satan. Still more, You have promised and reserved very great rewards for those who fear Your Name. Glory to You in the highest! Amen.

"Your wrath came, as did the time for the dead to be judged." This is the day of God's wrath, which will cause all to fear God. The judgment of the dead also comes, and this is a good thing. We have longed for fair judgment and for injustices to be mended. All will be set right by the very One who wipes away all tears from our eyes.

June 9 – Revelation 11:19

God's temple that is in heaven was opened, and the ark of the Lord's covenant was seen in his temple. Lightnings, sounds, thunders, an earthquake, and great hail followed.

What else happens at the seventh trumpet?

1.

2.

3.

4.

5.

Prayer: Father in heaven, we may forget, but You never do. Your covenant with Adam and Eve, Abraham, Isaac, Israel, and with us through Jesus Christ is ever before You in Your temple in heaven. We live for the hope of this day, the fulfillment of all of Your promises. Even so, come Lord Jesus! Amen.

The ark of the Lord's covenant was seen in his temple. In the first and second temples, the ark was hidden behind the veil and door to the temple and within the walls of the court. Jesus's death tore the veil and gave us access to God's throne. Here at His return the ark in heaven itself is visible, showing God is fulfilling His promises, written on tablets of stone.

June 10 - Revelation 12:1

A great sign was seen in heaven: a woman clothed with the sun, and the moon under her feet, and on her head a crown of twelve stars.

What did John see?

Where was this sign?

What were the elements of this sign?

1.

2.

3.

Prayer: Father, after You revealed the return of Jesus Christ, You now give a great sign or symbol in heaven. John recorded what he saw. Help us to understand Your sign and live accordingly. In Jesus's Name, we pray. Amen

A woman clothed with the sun, and the moon under her feet, and on her head a crown of twelve stars. The sign consists of a woman with the sun and moon and a crown of twelve stars. Each of these images means something. We must search the Scriptures carefully to understand, beginning with **Revelation 12.**

June 11 – Revelation 12:2

She was with child. She cried out in pain, laboring to give birth.

What happened to the woman?

1.

2.

3.

Who could this woman be?

Prayer: Father, the pain of a woman in childbirth is one of the most intense and common pains for mankind. Yet it is a pain that leads to the joy of a new person in the world. Help us to bear our pains, knowing You are creating a new person in us, and we, too, will experience great joy. In Jesus's Name, we pray. Amen.

She was with child. This sign has the elements of a good parable. A mysterious beginning, cloaked in symbols, a dramatic action, and then anticipation of what will come next.

June 12 – Revelation 12:3

Another sign was seen in heaven. Behold, a great red dragon, having seven heads and ten horns, and on his heads seven crowns.

What other sign appeared in heaven?

How was this sign described?

1.

2.

3.

4.

Prayer: Father, here we have more symbols to understand. Help us, great Lord Almighty, to see what each one means and to have the whole meaning of the parable given to us. In the Name of our Wisdom, Jesus Christ, we pray. Amen.

A great red dragon, having seven heads and ten horns. The hearers and readers of Revelation in John's day would identify this dragon with Daniel's four beasts in **Daniel** 7. By the first century, the meaning of the four beasts was plain: the empires of Babylon, Persia, Greece, and Rome. We need to be patient and study what meaning is meant here.

June 13 - Revelation 12:4

His tail drew one third of the stars of the sky, and threw them to the earth. The dragon stood before the woman who was about to give birth, so that when she gave birth he might devour her child.

What did the dragon do in the past?

Where did the dragon stand?

What did the dragon seek to do next?

Prayer: Father, there is always opposition to Your plans, whether from men or fallen angels. Help us to support You in Your work and not oppose You in what we say and do. In Jesus's Name, we pray. Amen.

His tail drew one third of the stars of the sky, and threw them to the earth. This statement rules out several theories of who this dragon is. It cannot be any human or empire, for humans cannot cast down stars, either literal or figurative. Remember Jesus said the seven stars in His right hand are seven angels. (See **Revelation 1:20**.)

June 14 - Revelation 12:5

She gave birth to a son, a male child, who is to rule all the nations with a rod of iron. Her child was caught up to God, and to his throne.

What were the characteristics of the male child the woman bore?

1.

2.

Who in history has these characteristics?

What historical time frame is bracketed by the events in verse 5?

Prayer: Ah, Father, it is amazing how You interfere with world history, as You did with Your Son Jesus Christ. He as God, came to Earth as a human man, taught and sacrificed, and rose again, all recorded by history. You impact us every day, to this day, Lord Jesus. Amen.

Her child was caught up to God, and to his throne. There is no room to interpret this child as anyone other than Jesus Christ.

John 3:13 *He said, "No one has ascended into heaven but he who descended out of heaven, the Son of Man, who is in heaven."*

This understanding means the woman is Mary, or, symbolically, Israel. Even more symbolically, she may represent Eve and all mankind, fulfilling God's promise that the woman's seed would crush the serpent. (See **Genesis 3:15**.)

June 15 – Revelation 12:6

The woman fled into the wilderness, where she has a place prepared by God, that there they may nourish her one thousand two hundred sixty days.

Where did the woman flee?

How long was the woman hidden?

Where is this action happening?

Prayer: Father, Your revelation has these visions cloaked in symbols and numerology. Help us to understand your symbols correctly and to take action now, according to Your will now, not according to our supposition. In Jesus's Name, we pray. Amen.

The woman fled into the wilderness, where she has a place prepared by God. This image evokes the history of Israel fleeing into the wilderness from the Egyptian army. The timeframe seems to be after Jesus's ascension to heaven, but before His second coming at the seventh trumpet. Notice how the woman transformed from a sign in heaven to a woman on Earth in the wilderness. Whatever explanation we adopt of this vision must explain this, too.

June 16 - Revelation 12:7

There was war in the sky. Michael and his angels made war on the dragon. The dragon and his angels made war.

What happened in heaven?

Who fought the war in heaven?

When did this happen, or is it in the future?

Prayer: Father, You are the Author of all knowledge, and You are revealing this to us. There is a war in heaven behind our wars on Earth. Help us to understand this and love all mankind. We are not warring with humanity but with spiritual darkness. Thank You, Jesus Christ, that You have already won the victory! Amen.

Michael and his angels made war on the dragon. Michael stands for Daniel's people.

Daniel 12:1 *"At that time Michael will stand up, the great prince who stands for the children of your people; and there will be a time of trouble, such as never was since there was a nation even to that same time. At that time your people will be delivered, everyone who is found written in the book."*

This is likely the same event as in **Revelation 12:7**, occurring before Jesus's return.

June 17 - Revelation 12:8

They didn't prevail. No place was found for them any more in heaven.

Who won the war in heaven?

How symbolic or literal is this war in heaven?

Why would Satan and his angels be cast out of heaven after having access for thousands of years? (See Job 1:6.)

Prayer: Father, thank You for leaving clues about these mysterious events and symbols throughout the Bible. Thank You for rewarding those who diligently search Your Scriptures and for hiding the truth from those who can't be bothered. Help us understand, for our insight is limited. In the Name of the Wisdom of God, Jesus Christ. Amen.

No place was found for them any more in heaven. At this point in the vision, Satan and his angels or demons have been cast out of heaven, with no access to God. When does this or will this occur? We must read further in Revelation.

June 18 – Revelation 12:9

The great dragon was thrown down, the old serpent, he who is called the devil and Satan, the deceiver of the whole world. He was thrown down to the earth, and his angels were thrown down with him.

Who is the dragon in this vision?

Who is the serpent in the garden of Eden?

What does he do to the world?

What happened to the devil after his defeat in heaven?

Prayer: Father, regardless of our limited understanding, this is a monumental change in the world and the universe: Satan and his demons have no access to You and are confined to the Earth. Lead us away from Satan's temptations, and deliver us from the evil he causes. In the Name of Almighty God, we pray. Amen.

The great dragon was thrown down, the old serpent, he who is called the devil and Satan, the deceiver of the whole world. This is a key verse in Revelation and the whole Bible: Satan is identified in all his guises: a dragon behind vicious governments, a serpent, who deceived Adam and Eve, a devil, a liar, and Satan, the adversary of God and mankind. We can use this verse to identify Satan's roles elsewhere in the Bible and prophecy.

June 19 – Revelation 12:10

I heard a loud voice in heaven, saying, "Now the salvation, the power, and the Kingdom of our God, and the authority of his Christ has come; for the accuser of our brothers has been thrown down, who accuses them before our God day and night."

What was announced from heaven?

1.

2.

3.

4.

5.

Have any of these events happened in the current day?

Prayer: Father, we long to know the "how" and "when" of Jesus's return and the arrival of Your kingdom to this Earth. Yet You only give us hints of what will happen, and You hide when it will occur. Help us to be content with Your revelation and to wait in faith for Jesus, filling our time with Your work until then. In the Name of our King, we pray. Amen.

For the accuser of our brothers has been thrown down, who accuses them before our God day and night. This is a startling statement, that Satan not only accuses Christians but does so continually before God. We have a vivid example in Job:

Job 1:9-11 *Then Satan answered Yahweh, and said, "Does Job fear God for nothing?*[10] *Haven't you made a hedge around him, and around his house, and around all that he has, on every side? You have blessed the work of his hands, and his substance is increased in the land.*[11] *But stretch out your hand now, and touch all that he has, and he will renounce you to your face."*

Satan is being a prosecuting attorney before God. Note he also charges God with unwarranted blessings that "bribe" Job into obedience. Read the book of Job to see how this turns out.

June 20 – Revelation 12:11

They overcame him because of the Lamb's blood, and because of the word of their testimony. They didn't love their life, even to death.

How did the brothers overcome Satan?

1.

2.

3.

Prayer: Lord Jesus, You warned us we must love You more than life itself. We must carry our cross daily for You, as You did for us. We lack the strength to overcome. Help us in our weaknesses to overcome all opposition and gain victory. Amen.

And because of the word of their testimony. Overcoming by the blood of the Lamb is a common theme in Christianity and is a lyric in many songs. But overcoming by the word of our testimony is rarely considered. All this means is we testify to others, persecutors in this case, of how God has saved us. This is very simple, for it is our own story of salvation. Yet it overcomes Satan.

June 21 – Revelation 12:12

"Therefore rejoice, heavens, and you who dwell in them. Woe to the earth and to the sea, because the devil has gone down to you, having great wrath, knowing that he has but a short time."

After Satan is cast from heaven, who rejoices?

Who has woe?

Why is Satan angry?

Prayer: Father, Satan persecutes us before Your throne in heaven. How much more will he do so when he is confined to the Earth and filled with great anger! Help us to bear any burden for the sake of Jesus and for our brethren who also suffer with us. Lord Jesus, we fix our eyes on You. Do not forsake us! Amen.

Knowing that he has but a short time. This is a key statement to placing these events in history and prophecy. When is Satan cast down? Why does he have just a short time? How long is that time? Once the end of this time is revealed, we can work backward to when he is cast down.

June 22 – Revelation 12:13

When the dragon saw that he was thrown down to the earth, he persecuted the woman who gave birth to the male child.

What did the dragon do on Earth?

Who is the woman in this persecution?

Prayer: Father, it doesn't matter who Satan persecutes. Let us oppose him. Let us come before Your throne on our knees in the Name of Jesus Christ to stop, frustrate, and thwart all the works of the devil. By Your power and might and Spirit we pray. Amen.

He persecuted the woman who gave birth to the male child. There were three possible meanings to this symbolic woman in verse 1: Mary; 2. Israel; 3. Eve and all mankind. Since this persecution takes place well after Jesus's ascension to heaven, and after Satan is expelled, we can rule out Mary. This could refer to Israel. The Jews have been persecuted for thousands of years to the present day. It could refer to the Christian church, which is also called Israel, having been grafted into Israel's olive tree, as Paul teaches. **Romans 11:13-24**. The Church is also called a woman multiple times in the New Testament.

June 23 – Revelation 12:14

Two wings of the great eagle were given to the woman, that she might fly into the wilderness to her place, so that she might be nourished for a time, and times, and half a time, from the face of the serpent.

What happens to the woman while she is under persecution?

How long was the woman in the wilderness?

Who gives the wings of the eagle and prepares a place in the wilderness for the woman?

Prayer: Ah Father, You know what we need before we ask. The woman needed to escape Satan's persecution, and You gave her wings. The woman needed a place to hide, and You gave her a place of nourishment. You did all these things without effort on her part, and we praise You for Your grace and mercy. Amen.

Two wings of the great eagle were given to the woman, that she might fly into the wilderness. Jews will immediately recognize this symbolism from the Song of Moses

Deuteronomy 32:10-11 *He found him in a desert land, in the waste howling wilderness. He surrounded him. He cared for him. He kept him as the apple of his eye.[11] As an eagle that stirs up her nest, that flutters over her young, he spread abroad his wings, he took them, he bore them on his feathers.*

This metaphor is also used in **Exodus 19:4** and **Isaiah 40:31**. Since John was a Jew, and his audience was familiar with the Old Testament, he likely intended a metaphorical meaning of "eagles' wings."

June 24 – Revelation 12:15

The serpent spewed water out of his mouth after the woman like a river, that he might cause her to be carried away by the stream.

How did the serpent attack the woman in the wilderness?

Is this literal water or a metaphor of some kind?

List out all the persecutions caused by Satan in this chapter to this point.

1.

2.

3.

4.

Prayer: Lord God, although we may be in over our heads and drowning, yet You will deliver us from evil. You made a way through the Red Sea and the Jordan. You will do so again. We praise You in the Name of Jesus! Amen.

The serpent spewed water out of his mouth after the woman like a river. This is a simile since the water is like a river. There are many psalms and prophecies about God delivering individuals from deep waters and floods. Also, the Bible compares armies to a flood. Like many prophecies, we will have to wait and see how the future fulfills this description.

June 26 - Revelation 12:16

The earth helped the woman, and the earth opened its mouth and swallowed up the river which the dragon spewed out of his mouth.

How was the woman defended in the wilderness?

What caused the Earth to help the woman?

Do you think this is a literal or figurative river?

Prayer: Father, help us live with uncertainty in our understanding and our knowledge of the future. Although You have revealed a lot, and we understand significant events that will happen in the future, the details are not clear. Help us to accept that we don't know and to be humble and wait upon You. In Jesus's Name, we pray. Amen.

The earth helped the woman, and the earth opened its mouth and swallowed up the river. Here we have a miracle: saving Israel and the Church from Satan's flood. God doesn't repeat Himself: with the Red Sea, the waters split at Moses's staff. With the Jordan, the waters withdrew when the priests' feet touched the Jordan. Here, the Earth opens up and swallows this river. We don't need to understand the details to praise God for the deliverance.

June 26 – Revelation 12:17

The dragon grew angry with the woman, and went away to make war with the rest of her offspring, who keep God's commandments and hold Jesus' testimony.

What did the dragon do after the woman escapes?

How does Revelation identify the rest of the woman's offspring?

1.

2.

When does this happen?

Prayer: Father, help us understand this parable, which began in **Revelation 12**. You recounted Jesus's birth and ascension to heaven, then a war in heaven, ending in Satan being cast to the Earth for a short time. Regardless of how much or how little we understand, help us to keep Your commandments and hold to Jesus's testimony. Amen.

With the rest of her offspring, who keep God's commandments and hold Jesus's testimony. Here we have a clear identification of the woman's offspring: Christians who hold Jesus's testimony and keep the commandments of God. Are we among that group?

June 27 - Revelation 13:1

Then I stood on the sand of the sea. I saw a beast coming up out of the sea, having ten horns and seven heads. On his horns were ten crowns, and on his heads, blasphemous names.

Where is John?

What does John see?

What is the appearance of the beast?

1.

2.

3.

4.

Prayer: Just when we begin to understand one symbol in Revelation, another one appears. Help us, Father, so that we are not overwhelmed by all You have put in this Book, but to patiently study each word until we understand. In the Name of the Word of God, we pray. Amen.

I saw a beast coming up out of the sea. Those who have read the book of Daniel will have an alarm go off in recognition of this vision. Compare it:

Daniel 7:2-3 *Daniel spoke and said, "I saw in my vision by night, and, behold, the four winds of the sky broke out on the great sea.³ Four great animals came up from the sea, different from one another."*

June 28 - Revelation 13:2

The beast which I saw was like a leopard, and his feet were like those of a bear, and his mouth like the mouth of a lion. The dragon gave him his power, his throne, and great authority.

What was the beast like?

What did the dragon give the beast?

1.

2.

3.

Prayer: Father, Your words are full of meaning, yet we can't fully grasp them. Help us to understand each word and to conform to the image of Jesus Christ. Amen.

The dragon gave him his power, his throne, and great authority. This is very much like Satan's third temptation of Jesus:

Matthew 4:8-9 *Again, the devil took him to an exceedingly high mountain, and showed him all the kingdoms of the world and their glory.⁹ He said to him, "I will give you all of these things, if you will fall down and worship me."*

Unlike Jesus, this beast seems to agree to the devil's terms.

June 29 – Revelation 13:3

One of his heads looked like it had been wounded fatally. His fatal wound was healed, and the whole earth marveled at the beast.

What surprising healing occurred?

How did the world react?

Why do you think this is so?

Prayer: Father, Jesus urged us to watch and be ready for His return at any time. Keep us safe from such deception that even Your elect Christians could be deceived, if it were possible. Empower us to watch the signs of the times and do Your work urgently, just as Jesus did in His short time on Earth. Amen.

One of his heads looked like it had been wounded fatally. The head may represent a king or a kingdom. It seemed dead, but it came back to life. Such a miracle will produce awe, wonder, and worship among the subjects of the kingdom and around the world.

June 30 – Revelation 13:4

They worshiped the dragon, because he gave his authority to the beast, and they worshiped the beast, saying, "Who is like the beast? Who is able to make war with him?"

What did the world do?

What did the world say?

Why did the world worship the beast?

Prayer: Father, we're quick to admire men and great accomplishments. The world loves a winner, and victors in war are praised. But You are the only winner, and Your Son Jesus is the unconquered King. Come soon, Lord Jesus! Amen.

They worshiped the dragon, because he gave his authority to the beast, and they worshiped the beast. In this sad prophecy, the whole world worships Satan and the world ruler who represents the devil.

July 1 – Revelation 13:5

A mouth speaking great things and blasphemy was given to him. Authority to make war for forty-two months was given to him.

How long did the beast's mouth speak blasphemies?

What else does the beast do during this time?

Where else have we seen this length of time in Revelation?

Prayer: Holy God, it is amazing You have allowed men to blaspheme Your Name as long as we have been on the Earth. Yet it is by such mercy that You have saved us, and You will save people even from this evil ruler. We praise You for Your grace in Jesus Christ! Amen.

Authority to make war for forty-two months was given to him. We see forty-two months again. This coincides with the forty-two months the woman is hidden in the wilderness in **Revelation 12:14**. Note that forty-two months is three-and-a-half years, using the Biblical lunar calendar. The Bible also calls this time "a time, times, and half a time." (See **Daniel 7:25** and **12:7**.)

July 2 – Revelation 13:6

He opened his mouth for blasphemy against God, to blaspheme his name, and his dwelling, those who dwell in heaven.

Who does the beast blaspheme?

1.

2.

3.

Why would the beast blaspheme God, heaven, and the heavenly dwellers?

Prayer: Father, it's amazing that You permit us and the devil to sin, even blaspheme Your Name. You record all things, and You will judge all through Jesus Christ, based on what we say and what we do. Help us to keep that in our minds, always. In the Name of God, Jesus Christ, we pray. Amen.

He opened his mouth for blasphemy against God. What is Satan's motive? He wishes to exalt himself over God and so denigrates God's Name.

Isaiah 14:12-14 *How you have fallen from heaven, shining one, son of the dawn! How you are cut down to the ground, who laid the nations low!* [13] *You said in your heart, "I will ascend into heaven! I will exalt my throne above the stars of God! I will sit on the mountain of assembly, in the far north!* [14] *I will ascend above the heights of the clouds! I will make myself like the Most High!"*

July 3 – Revelation 13:7

It was given to him to make war with the saints, and to overcome them. Authority over every tribe, people, language, and nation was given to him.

Against whom does the beast make war?

The beast has power over whom?

1.

2.

3.

4.

When does this war occur?

Prayer: Lord Jesus, You told us to be of good cheer for You have overcome the world. We rest in You, on Your Word, and we pray for endurance and strength in the middle of Satan's attacks. You are forever exalted, O God of glory! Amen.

It was given to him to make war with the saints. This war on the saints, the holy ones of God, echoes what was said earlier in Revelation.

Revelation 12:17 *The dragon grew angry with the woman, and went away to make war with the rest of her offspring, who keep God's commandments and hold Jesus' testimony.*

The two verses indicate this war is the same war, at the same time: after Satan and his demons are cast from heaven forever.

July 4 - Revelation 13:8

All who dwell on the earth will worship him, everyone whose name has not been written from the foundation of the world in the book of life of the Lamb who has been killed.

Who will worship the beast?

1.

2.

Who owns the Book of Life?

Who will not worship the beast?

Prayer: Thank You, Lord God, that our names are written in the Book of Life and that we are called to worship You. Help us expunge every bit of service and worship to anyone other than You! In the Name of the Lamb of God, Amen.

All who dwell on the earth will worship him, everyone whose name has not been written. We see the world will be split into two factions: those who worship Satan and those who worship God. Everyone will have to choose one side or the other.

July 5 – Revelation 13:9-10

If anyone has an ear, let him hear.[10] "If anyone leads into captivity, into captivity he goes. If anyone will kill with the sword, he must be killed with a sword." Here is the endurance and the faith of the saints.

What are the two parts of the warning?

1.

2.

What are God's saints told about this time?

Prayer: Father, You call us to endure with faith in the troubled times to come and now. We cannot; we lack the strength. We pray for the strength and endurance of Jesus Christ that we may pass this life-and-death test. In the Name of the Lamb of God, Amen.

If anyone has an ear, let him hear. This phrase is used for the first time since the seven letters to the seven churches. Imagine listening to this book for the first time in one of these congregations. You'd be caught up in the narrative and then this phrase would make you heed the next verse carefully.

July 6 – Revelation 13:11

And I saw another beast coming up out of the land, and it had two horns, like a lamb, and it was speaking as a dragon.

Where does the second beast come from?

What is the second beast like?

1.

2.

Who else appears as a lamb in Revelation?

What is the difference between the second beast and the Lamb of God?

Prayer: Lord Jesus, You alone are the Lamb of God. Help us so we are not deceived by any substitute, no matter what miracles they may perform. In Your Holy Name, we pray. Amen.

And it was speaking as a dragon. We know from **Revelation 12:9** that the dragon is Satan, the father of lies. This second beast is the one who comes with all deceitfulness, spoken of by Paul:

2 Thessalonians 2:8-12 *Then the lawless one will be revealed, whom the Lord will kill with the breath of His mouth, and destroy by the manifestation of His coming;[9] even he whose coming is according to the working of Satan with all power and signs and lying wonders,[10] and with all deception of wickedness for those who are being lost, because they didn't receive the love of the truth, that they might be saved.[11] Because of this, God sends them a working of error, that they should believe a lie;[12] that they all might be judged who didn't believe the truth, but had pleasure in unrighteousness.*

July 7 – Revelation 13:12

He exercises all the authority of the first beast in his presence. He makes the earth and those who dwell in it to worship the first beast, whose fatal wound was healed.

What does the second beast do?

1.

2.

Where does the second beast get his authority?

Where does the first beast get his authority?

Prayer: Father, the whole world follows and worships Satan. Help us so that we are not deceived, but help us cleave to Jesus Christ, the Word of God. Jesus, help us believe and follow Your word. Amen.

He makes the earth and those who dwell in it to worship the first beast. When you combine this with **Revelation 13:2,** "*The dragon gave him his power, his throne, and great authority,*" one realizes Satan's power, authority, and rulership is vested in the first beast. That means the world when it worships this beast, this man, is worshiping Satan, which is what Satan wants.

July 8 – Revelation 13:13

He performs great signs, even making fire come down out of the sky to the earth in the sight of people.

How does the second beast cause the Earth to worship the first beast?

1.

2.

Who else has the authority to call fire down from heaven?

Prayer: Father, Your angels, even Your fallen ones, are very powerful. Let us not be deceived to wander from You and Jesus, no matter how amazing the miracles may be. In Jesus's Name, we pray. Amen.

Even making fire come down out of the sky to the earth in the sight of people. This is a direct copy of the two witnesses' miracles, as well as Elijah's in **1 Kings 2:11-12**. The second beast may claim to be Elijah.

July 9 – Revelation 13:14

He deceives people who dwell on the earth because of the signs he was granted to do in front of the beast, saying to those who dwell on the earth that they should make an image to the beast who had the sword wound and lived.

What was the purpose of the signs performed by the second beast?

What does the second beast make the people do?

An image of the first beast is an image of what?

How was the first beast wounded?

Prayer: Jesus, You taught that those who live by the sword, die by the sword. Help us to be men and women of peace, even living with our enemies in peace. In the Name of the Price of Peace, we pray. Amen. (See **Matthew 26:52**.)

They should make an image to the beast who had the sword wound and lived. The beast may represent a government or the head of the government. In either case, death by sword is understood to be death in warfare. This head of government may appears to die in war, but he is seemingly brought back to life by Satan. It's no wonder the world worships him.

July 10 – Revelation 13:15

It was given to him to give breath to it, to the image of the beast, that the image of the beast should both speak, and cause as many as wouldn't worship the image of the beast to be killed.

What does the second beast cause the image to do?

1.

2.

What effects would these actions have on the people of the world?

Prayer: Once again, Father, we don't know the exact way these prophesies will be fulfilled, but help us to be watchful and aware when governments demand worship of their leaders and to not follow along with the crowd. In the Name of the King, we pray. Amen.

And cause as many as wouldn't worship the image of the beast to be killed. We've already had governments within the last century and currently today who will kill their citizens if their leader is not worshiped. Christians are recognized as a threat to the government and are imprisoned and killed. Are we willing to die for Christ?

July 11 – Revelation 13:16

He causes all, the small and the great, the rich and the poor, and the free and the slave, to be given marks on their right hands, or on their foreheads.

What does the second beast do?

Who is affected by the edict?

1.

2.

3.

4.

5.

6.

Prayer: Father in heaven, for so many people money is the center of their lives, and those who control money control people's lives. Let it not be so with us. Let us forsake wealth and money to follow You alone. In Jesus's Name, we pray. Amen.

He causes all, the small and the great, the rich and the poor, and the free and the slave, to be given marks. This practice has a historical basis. In Rome, during certain emperors, people were required to make an offering to the emperor. They would then get a marker indicating they had done so. Without this marker, no one could buy anything in any Roman town[17].

July 12 – Revelation 13:17

And that no one would be able to buy or to sell, unless he has that mark, which is the name of the beast or the number of his name.

What is the effect of the mark of the beast?

Whom did God mark with his seal on their foreheads in Revelation 7?

What is the effect of God's seal in Revelation 7?

Prayer: Father, we only have two choices in our lives: will we follow You and Jesus, or will we follow Satan? We love You and only want to follow You, but we're weak and fearful. Strengthen us with Your faith and courage so we may follow You alone. In Jesus's Name, we pray. Amen.

And that no one would be able to buy or to sell, unless he has that mark. Exactly how this will work, we don't know, but the intent is clear: tie obedience to the beast and Satan to our economy and our daily lives.

July 13 – Revelation 13:18

Here is wisdom. He who has understanding, let him calculate the number of the beast, for it is the number of a man. His number is six hundred sixty-six.

What is the number of the beast?

Why is the number used instead of the actual name of the beast?

Why is six hundred sixty-six the number of a man?

Prayer: Father, wisdom and understanding come from You. Grant us these things so that we may see through all deception and understand You and Your will clearly and then do them. In the Name of Wisdom, Jesus Christ, we pray. Amen.

... for it is the number of a man. His number is six hundred sixty-six. A popular belief about how to compute the number and what name it is to use the numeric values of Hebrew letters of "Nero Caesar," which adds to 666. The Greek version of "Nero Caesar" also becomes 666[17]. Some interpret this to mean John was imprisoned during Nero's reign, while others take it to refer obliquely to Domitian, the emperor who imprisoned John. Still others take it to refer to a future Roman emperor who is yet to appear. Like many prophecies, we must wait and see how God fulfills this.

July 14 – Revelation 14:1

I saw, and behold, the Lamb standing on Mount Zion, and with him a number, one hundred forty-four thousand, having his name, and the name of his Father, written on their foreheads.

Who is on Mount Zion in this vision?

1.

2.

What is written on the foreheads of the 144,000?

Where is Mount Zion?

Where is Jesus supposed to return?

Prayer: O Lord God, it is amazing You came into human history in a specific location through Jesus Christ. Even more amazing is that You gave the specific location of Your dwelling, Mount Zion, and the specific mount of Your return, the Mount of Olives. Thank You for touching human reality with Your flesh and blood and saving us. Amen.

I saw, and behold, the Lamb standing on Mount Zion. Mount Zion is also known as the Temple Mount and Mount Moriah. The fact of the Lamb standing there with His saints sets the time of the vision to after His return. Jesus's angel states He will return to the Mount of Olives in **Acts 1:11. Zechariah 14:4** also states that the Lord Yahweh will return to the Mount of Olives to fight His enemies. We know the place, but we don't know the time.

July 15 - Revelation 14:2

I heard a sound from heaven, like the sound of many waters, and like the sound of a great thunder. The sound which I heard was like that of harpists playing on their harps.

What did John hear?

1.

2.

3.

What do you think the sound was?

Prayer: Father, You're wonderful in giving us vivid descriptions of things we've never seen or heard before. You encourage us to use our imagination in picturing Your Kingdom to come. Then once it comes, You'll surprise us again. Thank You! Amen.

The sound which I heard was like that of harpists playing on their harps. Here we have a paradox: harps are typically soft and gentle in their sound, yet this sound is compared to a torrent and thunder. How can sound be both harp-like and thunderous? Such contradictions exist in God, too, Who is supremely powerful and gentle as well.

July 16 – Revelation 14:3

They sing a new song before the throne, and before the four living creatures and the elders. No one could learn the song except the one hundred forty-four thousand, those who had been redeemed out of the earth.

What was sung by the 144,000?

What was unique about the song?

Who are the 144,000?

Is this a literal 144,000 or figurative? Why?

Prayer: Father, the coming of Jesus Christ will be with great noise and with joyous singing. Each time we sing praise to You, Almighty God, help us remember we'll sing in Your Presence in the future. In Jesus's Name, we pray. Amen.

No one could learn the song except the one hundred forty-four thousand, those who had been redeemed out of the earth. Another paradox is here. We have a definite number: one hundred and forty-four thousand out of the twelve tribes of Israel. We also have a characteristic: those redeemed from the Earth. Jesus has redeemed billions of people since His appearance on Earth, of all nations. One explanation is the one hundred and forty-four thousand and the innumerable multitude are the same group from two perspectives: 1) One hundred and forty-four thousand are those saved from the Earth from Israel during the tribulation; 2) The innumerable multitude are those saved from all times and all nations. But both are saved and redeemed. There is no certain interpretation.

July 17 – Revelation 14:4-5

These are those who were not defiled with women, for they are virgins. These are those who follow the Lamb wherever he goes. These were redeemed by Jesus from among men, the first fruits to God and to the Lamb.[5] In their mouth was found no lie, for they are blameless.

What are the characteristics of the 144,000?

1.

2.

3.

4.

5.

Prayer: O Lord Jesus, You have made every Christian blameless by Your shed blood cleansing all our sins. You have redeemed us all. In response, we follow You wherever You go. Help us live up to our calling as Your firstfruits. Amen.

In their mouth was found no lie, for they are blameless. Another paradox appears: How can a human be blameless? Only by accepting Jesus's sacrifice as the offering for his or her sins. Jesus as God is of infinite worth, far more than all His creation. He voluntarily took on all the punishment for all the sins of His creation and died to pay for it all. In God, all paradoxes are resolved.

July 18 – Revelation 14:6

I saw an angel flying in mid heaven, having an eternal Good News to proclaim to those who dwell on the earth, and to every nation, tribe, language, and people.

What did the angel preach?

Where did the angel fly?

Who heard the message?

1.

2.

3.

4.

5.

What time in the future is this?

Why did God use an angel to preach the gospel at this time?

Prayer: Father, You are so loving You do not want a single person to be lost, but for all to come to repentance. Even when the church is completely glorified after Jesus's return, You still proclaim the gospel to those remaining, that some might be saved. Your gospel cannot be censored when Your angel preaches it aloud. Everyone in every language will understand. You are forever just and loving! Amen.

I saw an angel flying in mid heaven. The phrase "mid heaven" occurs only in Revelation, and we saw it earlier in Revelation:

Revelation 8:3 *I saw, and I heard an eagle, flying in mid heaven, saying with a loud voice, "Woe! Woe! Woe for those who dwell on the earth, because of the other voices of the trumpets of the three angels, who are yet to sound!"*

In Revelation 8:3, it was a warning to the people of the Earth. In **Revelation 14:6**, it is the gospel. In both cases, the speech was audible to people on Earth.

July 19 – Revelation 14:7

He said with a loud voice, "Fear the Lord, and give him glory; for the hour of his judgment has come. Worship him who made the heaven, the earth, the sea, and the springs of waters!"

What does the angel command?

1.

2.

3.

Why are these commanded?

Prayer: Father, You in Your wisdom know when and how to draw each person to Yourself. Some are called early and some late. You tailor Your calling for each person. May everyone come to repentance at the proper time. In Jesus's Name, the Creator of heaven and Earth, we pray. Amen.

Fear the Lord, and give him glory...Worship Him. It is interesting to compare the angel's message with what Jesus taught the apostles:

Mark 16:15-16 *"Go into all the world, and preach the Good News to the whole creation.[16] He who believes and is baptized will be saved; but he who disbelieves will be condemned."*

July 20 – Revelation 14:8

Another, a second angel, followed, saying, "Babylon the great has fallen, which has made all the nations to drink of the wine of the wrath of her sexual immorality."

What does another angel proclaim?

Why does this announced event happen?

Why does the angel tell this to the world?

Prayer: Lord God Almighty, You proclaim the good news of the fall of the evil empire of Babylon, which has ruled over men since the original Babylon. This removes the idol and the god men have worshiped instead of You. Let all fall and worship You alone! Amen.

"Babylon the great has fallen, which has made all the nations to drink of the wine of the wrath of her sexual immorality." Sexual immorality is rampant in society today, yet there may be another meaning to this. Israel's sins against God were compared to adultery for they were married to God at Mount Sinai. How much more so those who claim to be Christian and yet are unfaithful to God?

July 21 - Revelation 14:9

Another angel, a third, followed them, saying with a great voice, "If anyone worships the beast and his image, and receives a mark on his forehead, or on his hand…"

What does the third angel warn of?

1.

2.

3.

Why is the warning coming now?

Prayer: O Father, over and over You warn us about idolatry, worshiping things that are not You, that are not God. Once we worship, we obey. If we obey anyone but You, we destroy ourselves. Save us from false worship, now and into the future! You alone are God, Father, Son, and Holy Spirit. Amen.

If anyone worships the beast and his image, and receives a mark on his forehead, or on his hand. This mark indicates you are approved by the beast, that you have worshipped the beast adequately, and that you're good enough to live. Remember the beast represents Satan, who saves by works alone. This is fear-based religion. A person worships to save their life. God wants us to worship Him by giving up our lives.

July 22 – Revelation 14:10

He also will drink of the wine of the wrath of God, which is prepared unmixed in the cup of his anger. He will be tormented with fire and sulfur in the presence of the holy angels, and in the presence of the Lamb.

What is the punishment for worshiping the beast?

Why is the punishment so severe, after three-and-a-half years of beast worship?

What time is this in the future?

Prayer: Father, You are incredibly merciful, giving the wicked time to repent, but at some time punishment comes. When we see our sins, let us repent immediately and not wait to be punished for our sins. Help us to have gentle and humble hearts before You every day. In the Name of the gentle Son, we pray. Amen.

He also will drink of the wine of the wrath of God. The wrath of God descends upon these worshippers of the beast. This is after Jesus's return to the Earth. The worshippers, the beast, and Satan are all on the Earth. It seems likely the fire and brimstone will also be upon the Earth, somewhere.

Jeremiah 25:15-16 *For thus says the Lord God of Israel to me: "Take this wine cup of fury from My hand, and cause all the nations, to whom I send you, to drink it.¹⁶ And they will drink and stagger and go mad because of the sword that I will send among them."*

July 23 – Revelation 14:11

The smoke of their torment goes up forever and ever. They have no rest day and night, those who worship the beast and his image, and whoever receives the mark of his name.

What ascends forever?

What happens to the worshippers of the beast?

1.

2.

Prayer: Father, we trust in Your justice. As horrible as this punishment seems to be, we know all Your work, evil with the rebellious evildoers, will serve to bring mankind to You. We know the whole Earth will fear You, Jesus, which is just, for You are fearsome and not to be fought. Let Your will be done, Almighty God. Amen.

They have no rest day and night, those who worship the beast. This statement indicates that as long as people worship the beast, they will be tormented. Will people continue to receive the mark of the beast after Jesus's return? We don't know for sure. The time until the beast is destroyed after Jesus's return is not clear.

July 24 – Revelation 14:12

Here is the perseverance of the saints, those who keep the commandments of God, and the faith of Jesus.

How are the saints identified?

1.

2.

3.

Prayer: Father, we want to be among those numbered as saints. Help us to persevere even to death, guide us to keep the commandments of God, and enable us to hold on to the faith of Jesus. In His Name, we pray. Amen.

Here is the perseverance of the saints. God defines His saints in this verse: Those who keep His commandments and the faith of Jesus with perseverance. God is drawing a very clear line between His saints and those who follow the beast. No one will be allowed to sit on the fence.

July 25 – Revelation 14:13

I heard a voice from heaven saying, "Write, 'Blessed are the dead who die in the Lord from now on.'"

"Yes," says the Spirit, "that they may rest from their labors; for their works follow with them."

What is the blessing on those who die in the Lord?

When is this blessing issued?

Who are physical Christians on Earth at this time?

Prayer: Father, Your work of salvation never ends. You saved people before Jesus came. You saved many after the church was formed. And You will continue to save people after Jesus returns. Help us to labor for Your Kingdom forever! Amen.

"Blessed are the dead who die in the Lord from now on." Who are these blessed dead? What is "from now on"? It's a puzzle until we remember the timeline of this prophecy. Jesus just returned with the seventh trumpet. At that point, all Christians, living and dead, became glorified with spirit bodies like Jesus's. Who is Christian at this time, after Jesus's return? Those who converted in Jerusalem (See **Revelation 11:13**.) and elsewhere around the world after Jesus's return. The beast's power is still present on the earth and still killing Christians. These are the ones who are blessed "from now on." This blessing may extend to all Christians who die under Jesus's millennial rule.

July 26 – Revelation 14:14

I looked, and saw a white cloud, and on the cloud one sitting like a son of man, having on his head a golden crown, and in his hand a sharp sickle.

When is the harvest of the Earth?

Who harvests the Earth?

What is harvested?

Prayer: Lord Jesus, we are the fruit of Your labor, both when You lived and died on our behalf, and in Your resurrected life and work in the church ever after. You will come to Your own and gather us into Your arms where we'll remain forever. Thank You with all our hearts! Amen.

And on the cloud one sitting like a son of man. "Son of man" is Jesus's favorite name for Himself in the gospels.

Daniel 7:13-14 *"I saw in the night visions, and behold, there came with the clouds of the sky one like a son of man, and he came even to the ancient of days, and they brought him near before him.14 Dominion was given him, and glory, and a kingdom, that all the peoples, nations, and languages should serve him. His dominion is an everlasting dominion, which will not pass away, and his kingdom one that which will not be destroyed."*

July 27 – Revelation 14:15

Another angel came out of the temple, crying with a loud voice to him who sat on the cloud, "Send your sickle, and reap; for the hour to reap has come; for the harvest of the earth is ripe!"

Who calls for the harvest?

What is the ripe harvest?

Why harvest the Earth?

Prayer: Holy Father, You have sowed Your seed through Jesus, and You will surely reap Your harvest of Christians in the proper time. You care for Your crop and watch over them, and You will store Your harvest forever. We praise You for Your great work on this Earth. In Jesus's Name, we pray. Amen.

"For the harvest of the earth is ripe!" Jesus's parable of the wheat and the tares clearly explains this passage:

Matthew 13:38-40 *the field is the world, the good seeds are the children of the Kingdom, and the darnel weeds are the children of the evil one.39 The enemy who sowed them is the devil. The harvest is the end of the age, and the reapers are angels.40 As therefore the darnel weeds are gathered up and burned with fire; so will it be at the end of this age.*

July 28 – Revelation 14:16

He who sat on the cloud thrust his sickle on the earth, and the earth was reaped.

When does this happen?

Is this event within the timeline of Revelation 11, or is it a flashback to an earlier time?

How long does this reaping take?

Prayer: Father, it's to Your glory to conceal a matter. You told us Jesus would come as a suffering servant to die for our sins, and no one believed Your word. Now You reveal events before and after Jesus's second coming as King, and again we're confused. Clear away our confusion and help us to have steady faith in You to the day Jesus returns. In the Name of our King, we pray. Amen.

The earth was reaped. This harvest by Christ is of all Christians. Paul expands upon this event.

I Corinthians 15:51-54 *Behold, I tell you a mystery. We will not all sleep, but we will all be changed,[52] in a moment, in the twinkling of an eye, at the last trumpet. For the trumpet will sound and the dead will be raised incorruptible, and we will be changed.[53] For this perishable body must become imperishable, and this mortal must put on immortality.[54] But when this perishable body will have become imperishable, and this mortal will have put on immortality, then what is written will happen: "Death is swallowed up in victory."*

July 29 – Revelation 14:17

Another angel came out of the temple which is in heaven. He also had a sharp sickle.

What will the angel harvest?

Why are there two separate harvests?

Why is it an angel and not Jesus in this second harvest?

Prayer: Jesus, before we put our faith in You, we were dreading being in this second harvest of the wicked. Thank You, God Almighty, that You have removed our sin, and we can stand before You without condemnation. Amen.

Another angel came out of the temple which is in heaven. He also had a sharp sickle. Again, nothing explains this verse as well as Jesus's explanation of the parable of the wheat and the tares.

Matthew 13:38-39 *the field is the world, the good seeds are the children of the Kingdom, and the darnel weeds are the children of the evil one.[39] The enemy who sowed them is the devil. The harvest is the end of the age, and the reapers are angels.*

July 30 – Revelation 14:18

Another angel came out from the altar, he who has power over fire, and he called with a great voice to him who had the sharp sickle, saying, "Send your sharp sickle, and gather the clusters of the vine of the earth, for the earth's grapes are fully ripe!"

What is the meaning of this grape harvest?

What is the significance of "fully ripe"?

What does this grape harvest symbolize?

Prayer: O Father, how dreadful is Your judgment. You patiently wait, giving even the most evil men and women time to repent, with many opportunities. But when the evil ones are wholly devoted to evil, You deem them ripe for their just punishment, which falls more swiftly than anyone can imagine. Jesus, lead people to repentance, we pray. Amen.

For the earth's grapes are fully ripe! Consider what God said to Abraham as He made a covenant with him.

Genesis 15:13-16 *Then He said to Abram: "Know certainly that your descendants will be strangers in a land that is not theirs, and will serve them, and they will afflict them four hundred years.[14] And also the nation whom they serve I will judge; afterward they shall come out with great possessions.[15] Now as for you, you shall go to your fathers in peace; you shall be buried at a good old age.[16] But in the fourth generation they shall return here, for the iniquity of the Amorites is not yet complete."*

God, in judging the Amorites, allowed them to sin for four hundred years while Israel was in Egypt. Then their sin was full, and their destruction had come. In judging all the Earth, God has given even more time for repentance. But judgment will come upon all the wicked.

July 31 – Revelation 14:19

The angel thrust his sickle into the earth, and gathered the vintage of the earth, and threw it into the great wine press of the wrath of God.

What was harvested?

Where was the harvest thrown?

Who is under the wrath of God?

Prayer: Father, Your wrath is awesome and terrible. Let us shelter in Your Rock, Jesus Christ, so we may escape through His sacrifice and mercy. In His Name, we pray. Amen

The great wine press of the wrath of God. Jesus Christ is the escape from the wrath of God:

John 3:36 *"One who believes in the Son has eternal life, but one who disobeys the Son won't see life, but the wrath of God remains on him."*

Perhaps surprising to some, Jesus Christ Himself treads the winepress of the wrath of God:

Revelation 19:15 *Out of his mouth proceeds a sharp, double-edged sword, that with it he should strike the nations. He will rule them with an iron rod. He treads the wine press of the fierceness of the wrath of God, the Almighty.*

August 1 – Revelation 14:20

The wine press was trodden outside of the city, and blood came out of the wine press, even to the bridles of the horses, as far as one thousand six hundred stadia[13].

What happened to the grapes?

What is literal and what is figurative in this picture?

When does the wrath of God occur?

Prayer: Holy Father, by hiding the time of Jesus's return, You also hide the time of the world's judgment by Him. Humanity continues to live as if You don't exist and acts according to their desires. Help us to surrender to You now and live by Your desire. In Jesus's Name, we pray. Amen.

The wine press was trodden outside of the city, and blood came out of the wine press. This juxtaposition of wine with blood happens with communion, which symbolizes Jesus's blood. Now God pictures the blood of the wicked as wine in a press. This event is also mentioned in Isaiah.

Isaiah 63:4-6 *"For the day of vengeance was in my heart, and the year of my redeemed has come.[5] I looked, and there was no one to help; and I wondered that there was no one to uphold. Therefore my own arm brought salvation to me. My own wrath upheld me.[6] I trod down the peoples in my anger and made them drunk in my wrath. I poured their lifeblood out on the earth."*

---

[13] 1600 stadia = 296 kilometers or 184 miles

August 2 – Revelation 15:1

I saw another great and marvelous sign in the sky: seven angels having the seven last plagues, for in them God's wrath is finished.

What fulfills God's wrath?

Who carries the seven plagues?

Is this part of the seventh trumpet?

Is this part of the seventh seal?

Prayer: O holy Father, You reveal a little of your judgments at a time, in different pieces at various times. Let's not become overwhelmed by Your revelations, but instead faithfully follow Jesus Christ our Savior, Lord, and Judge. In His Name, we pray. Amen.

The seven last plagues, for in them God's wrath is finished.

John 19:30 When Jesus therefore had received the vinegar, he said, "It is finished." Then he bowed his head, and gave up his spirit.

Just as Jesus's death and sacrifice ended sin and death, so these last plagues end God's wrath on mankind for our sin and rebellion.

August 3 – Revelation 15:2

I saw something like a sea of glass mixed with fire, and those who overcame the beast, his image, and the number of his name, standing on the sea of glass, having harps of God.

Who stands on the sea of glass mixed with fire?

What do they have?

Where have we seen a large number of overcomers before the throne of God earlier in Revelation?

Prayer: Holy God, our death is never pleasant to consider, yet You have conquered death, Jesus. You have guaranteed our continued life beyond death. Help us not to fear death anymore, but to embrace You, Almighty God. Amen.

Those who overcame the beast, his image, and the number of his name, standing on the sea of glass. This is clear that these people in heaven are those who resisted the beast's power on Earth. We read about this earlier in Revelation:

Revelation 7:9,14-15 *After these things I looked, and behold, a great multitude, which no man could count, out of every nation and of all tribes, peoples, and languages, standing before the throne and before the Lamb, dressed in white robes, with palm branches in their hands.[14]*

And he said to me, These are they which came out of great tribulation, and have washed their robes, and made them white in the blood of the Lamb.[15] Therefore are they before the throne of God, and serve him day and night in his temple: and he that sitteth on the throne shall dwell among them. (KJV)

August 4 – Revelation 15:3

They sang the song of Moses, the servant of God, and the song of the Lamb, saying, "Great and marvelous are your works, Lord God, the Almighty! Righteous and true are your ways, you King of the nations."

What do they sing?

What are the words of the song of the Lamb?

1.

2.

Prayer: Lord God Almighty, just as You delivered Israel from Egypt through plagues and miracles, so You will deliver Your people on Earth from the beast's power. Help us so we never fear what man can do, but to love You with perfect love. Amen.

Righteous and true are your ways, you King of the nations. Jesus as the King of the nations judges the nations. The wicked He punishes, according to the truth of His word.

August 5 - Revelation 15:4

"Who wouldn't fear you, Lord, and glorify your name? For you only are holy. For all the nations will come and worship before you. For your righteous acts have been revealed."

What other verses are in the song of the Lamb?

1.

2.

3.

4.

Prayer: O Lord God, mankind has ignored and insulted You for thousands of years. Now is the time to praise You. Everyone will see how they have erred, and they will come and worship You. Speed this day, Almighty God! Amen.

For all the nations will come and worship before you. Here is a radical change in the world. Why? Jesus Christ is now ruling. The starving are fed. The sick are healed. The wicked are punished. Justice is done. Who wouldn't want to worship the King?

August 6 – Revelation 15:5

After these things I looked, and the temple of the tabernacle of the testimony in heaven was opened.

What happened next?

Where was this?

What earthly event caused the heavenly temple to be opened?

Prayer: Eternal Father, You directed the veil of the holy of holies to be torn at the death of Your Son. Far beyond His death, His return to rule the Earth opens the heavenly holy of holies. Let all rejoice as the salvation of the world begins in earnest. Amen.

The temple of the tabernacle of the testimony in heaven was opened. The implication was that the holy of holies in heaven was closed and even the angels could not see inside. Here is the corresponding earthly event in Matthew.

Matthew 27:50-51 *And Jesus cried out again with a loud voice, and yielded up His spirit.*[51] *Behold, the veil of the temple was torn in two from the top to the bottom. The earth quaked and the rocks were split.*

August 7 – Revelation 15:6

The seven angels who had the seven plagues came out, clothed with pure, bright linen, and wearing golden sashes around their breasts.

Why was the heavenly Temple opened?

Who came out?

How did the angels appear?

1.

2.

Prayer: How glorious You are, God Almighty, that the most powerful angels carrying out Your judgments are clothed in beauty. Let all the angels and all mankind praise You, in Jesus's Name. Amen.

The seven angels who had the seven plagues came out. These angels were in the temple of God in heaven. The implication is that God Himself selected them for this job.

August 8 – Revelation 15:7

One of the four living creatures gave to the seven angels seven golden bowls full of the wrath of God, who lives forever and ever.

What did the angels receive?

Who gave the angels the bowls?

Do you think the seven bowls will be worse than the seven trumpets or the seven seals?

Prayer: Holy Father, You give us great detail about Your coming judgments upon the Earth and mankind. Help us remember that You correct people to lead them to repentance. The harsher the correction, the more it takes to cause the repentance. You also provide salvation to all who repent. In Jesus's Name, we praise You for Your justice. Amen.

One of four living creatures gave to the seven angels seven golden bowls full of the wrath of God. One of the four seraphim give the bowls of the wrath of God to the seven angels chosen by God. He delegates His judgments and punishments to His angels to carry out. Compare this with the punishments of Sodom and Gomorrah in **Genesis 19** and Egypt in **Exodus 6-14** which were carried out by angels.

August 9 – Revelation 15:8

The temple was filled with smoke from the glory of God, and from his power. No one was able to enter into the temple until the seven plagues of the seven angels would be finished.

What happened to God's temple in heaven?

What was the result of this event?

Why did this event happen?

Prayer: Ah, Lord God! Who can stand in the intensity of Your Presence? Not the high priest on Earth nor the angels in heaven can enter Your temple without Your permission. Let us treasure our prayers in Jesus's Name, which allow us to go to Your very throne. Amen.

The temple was filled with smoke from the glory of God, and from his power. Again, this event echoes similar events in the Old Testament, when the tabernacle and the temple were dedicated. The glory of God filled the earthly temple, and the priests could not enter. What is being dedicated now? Perhaps it is the whole Earth being dedicated to God.

August 10 - Revelation 16:1

I heard a loud voice out of the temple, saying to the seven angels, "Go and pour out the seven bowls of the wrath of God on the earth!"

What command came out of the temple?

Who spoke this command?

Where was the wrath of God to be poured out?

Prayer: Lord God, from the beginning You have sought to make heaven on Earth through humanity. You allowed humanity to resist You to this point, but now that time ends. You cannot be resisted. Your will cannot be thwarted. Glory to You forever! Amen.

I heard a loud voice out of the temple. This may be the very voice of God Himself. Only He can initiate these final punishments.

August 11 – Revelation 16:2

The first went, and poured out his bowl into the earth, and it became a harmful and evil sore on the people who had the mark of the beast, and who worshiped his image.

What was the first plague upon the Earth?

Upon whom did this plague fall?

Who didn't receive this plague?

Prayer: Father in heaven, we hate pain and suffering, but all too often we bring it on ourselves through our actions. Help us to change now before we suffer the consequences of our sins. In Jesus's Name, we pray. Amen.

And it became a harmful and evil sore on the people who had the mark of the beast. The scope of this plague is limited to those who worship the beast. The beast tried to get everyone on Earth to worship him, but he only had three-and-a-half years, so some people were outside this system.

August 12 – Revelation 16:3

The second angel poured out his bowl into the sea, and it became blood as of a dead man. Every living thing in the sea died.

What was the second plague upon the Earth?

Upon whom did this plague fall?

Who didn't receive this plague?

Prayer: Father, we have abused the Earth with pollution and destruction for thousands of years. We have sown salt in the land, we have deforested it, we have overgrazed it, and we have hunted animals to extinction. Now we reap the full consequences of our actions with the destruction of all life in the sea. Save us, O Lord, from ourselves! Amen.

Every living thing in the sea died. This plague is breathtaking in scope. Like the Nile turning to blood in ancient Egypt, everything dies in the sea: all plankton, all fish, all whales, everything. This is nothing less than the destruction of our ecosystem.

August 13 – Revelation 16:4

The third poured out his bowl into the rivers and springs of water, and they became blood.

What was the second plague upon the Earth?

Upon whom did this plague fall?

Who didn't receive this plague?

Prayer: Save us from our sins, Almighty God! Our sins have consequences beyond ourselves, Every person on Earth is affected. We have hope in salvation in Jesus, both of our souls and the Earth. Amen.

The rivers and springs of water, and they became blood. Now, in addition to no food from the sea, there is no water to drink nor fish from the fresh water. The only sources remaining may be glacial ice and underground aquifers. The world will not last long in this state.

August 14 – Revelation 16:5-6

I heard the angel of the waters saying, "You are righteous, who are and who were, O Holy One, because you have judged these things.⁶ For they poured out the blood of saints and prophets, and you have given them blood to drink. They deserve this."

Who praises God after the third plague?

Why is God just to punish mankind like this?

Who is punished?

Prayer: Father, mankind's sins are horrifying, and Your punishments fit the crime. They have killed Your saints and prophets and committed bloody crimes, and now they have blood to drink. O lead people to repentance now! In the Name of our Savior, Amen.

"You are righteous, who are and who were, O Holy One, because you have judged these things." Something that can be lost in these horrible plagues is that these are Jesus's judgments. The Father has given all judgment to the Son. If people do not accept the Son as Savior, they will accept Jesus's judgments on them.

John 5:21-23 *For as the Father raises the dead and gives them life, even so the Son also gives life to whom he desires.²² For the Father judges no one, but he has given all judgment to the Son,²³ that all may honor the Son, even as they honor the Father. He who doesn't honor the Son doesn't honor the Father who sent him.*

August 15 – Revelation 16:7

I heard the altar saying, "Yes, Lord God, the Almighty, true and righteous are your judgments."

Who is praising God's judgments?

Is this the altar itself or someone else?

Who was under the altar in Revelation 6:9-10?

Prayer: Father, You and Jesus are united in Your judgments. The end of man's world has come, and those who resist the rule of Jesus are punished. Since these were the ones who caused the tribulation of Your saints, they receive their just reward. Let all praise You for Your justice and fear Your power! In Jesus's Name, we pray. Amen.

I heard the altar. This rather mysterious statement may be explained earlier in Revelation:

Revelation 6:9-10 *When he opened the fifth seal, I saw underneath the altar the souls of those who had been killed for the Word of God, and for the testimony of the Lamb which they had.[10] They cried with a loud voice, saying, "How long, Master, the holy and true, until you judge and avenge our blood on those who dwell on the earth?"*

This could also be an angel from the altar.

August 16 - Revelation 16:8

The fourth poured out his bowl on the sun, and it was given to him to scorch men with fire.

What was the fourth plague upon the Earth?

Upon whom did this plague fall?

Who didn't receive this plague?

Prayer: Father, all the blessings You gave mankind through Jesus Christ at creation are now turned to curses. We easily think we can live without You, when in fact, we're dependent upon You. Help us to realize our need for You every day. In Jesus our Creator, we pray. Amen.

The sun, and it was given to him to scorch men with fire. The sun is so powerful, it can easily destroy our planet. Yet we do not appreciate the delicate balance of power it contains and its unusually steady energy output. Nor do we give credit to God for making it so. The least nudge from God and the sun becomes destructive, instead of life-giving.

August 17 – Revelation 16:9

People were scorched with great heat, and people blasphemed the name of God who has the power over these plagues. They didn't repent and give him glory.

How did people react to this plague?

1.

2.

3.

Why didn't people repent before God?

Prayer: Father, we whom You've called and chosen have responded to Your call and have become Your sons and daughters. We often forget that it was Your initiative and pull that drew us to You and that without Your intervention, we had no desire to seek You. Let us remain humble before You and continue to pray for our enemies' repentance. Amen.

They didn't repent and give him glory. God has focused His plagues upon those who refuse to worship Him, who'd rather worship the beast and Satan. The intensity of plagues increases, to make people turn from their sins to Him. Yet their hearts are set against God, just as the Pharoah in Egypt was.

August 18 – Revelation 16:10

The fifth poured out his bowl on the throne of the beast, and his kingdom was darkened. They gnawed their tongues because of the pain.

What was the fifth plague upon the Earth?

Upon whom did this plague fall?

Who didn't receive this plague?

Prayer: Lord Jesus, You will never leave nor forsake us. You've given us the Holy Spirit to guide us. Lead us away from the kingdom of the beast so we will not suffer its plagues. In Your Name, we pray. Amen.

The fifth poured out his bowl on the throne of the beast, and his kingdom was darkened. This is identical to the ninth plague of Egypt.

Exodus 11:21-23 *Yahweh said to Moses, "Stretch out your hand toward the sky, that there may be darkness over the land of Egypt, even darkness which may be felt."²² Moses stretched out his hand toward the sky, and there was a thick darkness in all the land of Egypt for three days.²³ They didn't see one another, and nobody rose from his place for three days; but all the children of Israel had light in their dwellings.*

August 19 – Revelation 16:11

And they blasphemed the God of heaven because of their pains and their sores. They still didn't repent of their works.

What was the reaction of people to this plague?

1.

2.

Prayer: Father, You inflicted the sun on humanity, and they didn't repent. You inflict darkness upon them, and they still don't humble themselves before You. Help us all to repent before You now, so we may be saved now. In Jesus's Name, we pray. Amen.

They still didn't repent of their works. The reaction of those who refuse to repent to God may be anger toward God, as shown by their blasphemy or gnashing of teeth. The other reaction may be self-pity — sorry that they were caught in their sin, but not sorry for their sin. Jesus taught this in Matthew:

Matthew 13:41-42 *The Son of Man will send out his angels, and they will gather out of his Kingdom all things that cause stumbling and those who do iniquity,*[42] *and will cast them into the furnace of fire. There will be weeping and gnashing of teeth.*

August 20 – Revelation 16:12

The sixth poured out his bowl on the great river, the Euphrates. Its water was dried up, that the way might be prepared for the kings that come from the sunrise.

What happens at the sixth plague?

Why did this happen?

Where will these kings come from?

Prayer: O Father, we make our plans and schemes, yet You steer them to accomplish Your purposes. Help us to remember that Your will is to be done and not our own and to be humble before You. In Jesus's Name, we pray. Amen

That the way might be prepared for the kings that come from the sunrise. The river Euphrates will dry up, allowing kings to invade the Middle East from the east. We don't know which countries these will be, but Iran, Pakistan, India, and China are to the east.

August 21 – Revelation 16:13

I saw coming out of the mouth of the dragon, and out of the mouth of the beast, and out of the mouth of the false prophet, three unclean spirits, something like frogs.

What comes from the mouth of the dragon, the beast, and the false prophet?

The second plague of Egypt was a frog infestation. Is there a connection with this symbol?

Prayer: Father, You tell the truth. If Your Scripture uses an unclean animal to represent a spirit, then the spirit is unclean. Help us to remain clean in Jesus and not follow after anything else! In Jesus's Name, we pray. Amen.

Three unclean spirits, something like frogs. Frogs are unclean animals and so can represent unclean spirits. The second plague of Egypt was a plague of frogs. One of Egypt's gods was a frog. There may have been an evil spirit behind that frog worship.

August 22 – Revelation 16:14

For they are spirits of demons, performing signs; which go out to the kings of the whole inhabited earth, to gather them together for the war of that great day of God, the Almighty.

What do the frogs represent?

What do these unclean spirits do?

Why do they do these things?

Prayer: Father, not only do You use the plans of men, but the evil plans of demons also serve Your purposes. You desire all the nations who oppose the rule of Jesus to be gathered together, and so it will be done. Help us so that we are not deceived by the lies of Satan, now or in the future. In Jesus's Name, we pray. Amen.

Spirits of demons, performing signs; which go out to the kings of the whole inhabited earth The spirits use their power to incite kings to gather to fight Jesus, Who is ruling in Jerusalem.

August 23 – Revelation 16:15

"Behold, I come like a thief. Blessed is he who watches, and keeps his clothes, so that he doesn't walk naked, and they see his shame."

Who is speaking? How do we know?

To whom is He speaking?

To what does He refer?

Why is He speaking now?

What time is this?

Prayer: Thank You, Great Lord Almighty, that even in a world riven by war and disaster You give blessings and teaching to those who follow and obey Christ. So You clothe Your people in bravery, faith, steadfastness, and endurance in the face of opposition. Thank You for Your tender loving care. Amen.

Blessed is he who watches, and keeps his clothes. Jesus has already spoken to His church about clothing:

Revelation 3:4-5 *Nevertheless you have a few names in Sardis that didn't defile their garments. They will walk with me in white, for they are worthy.⁵ He who overcomes will be arrayed in white garments, and I will in no way blot his name out of the book of life, and I will confess his name before my Father, and before his angels.*

Revelation 3:18 *I counsel you to buy from me gold refined by fire, that you may become rich; and **white garments**, that you may clothe yourself, and that the shame of your nakedness may not be revealed; and eye salve to anoint your eyes, that you may see.*

This time is after His return, and these are new Christians, converted since the seventh trumpet. They need to know the importance of being clothed in His righteousness.

August 24 – Revelation 16:16

He gathered them together into the place which is called in Hebrew, "Megiddo."

Where do the kings and the armies of the Earth gather?

Where is this place located?

Why does He gather them there?

Prayer: Father, we have heard about Armageddon for many years, and it has become part of our culture. But it is an actual place, and a real battle will take place there. Help us to stay aligned with You and not fight against You. In Jesus's Name, we pray. Amen.

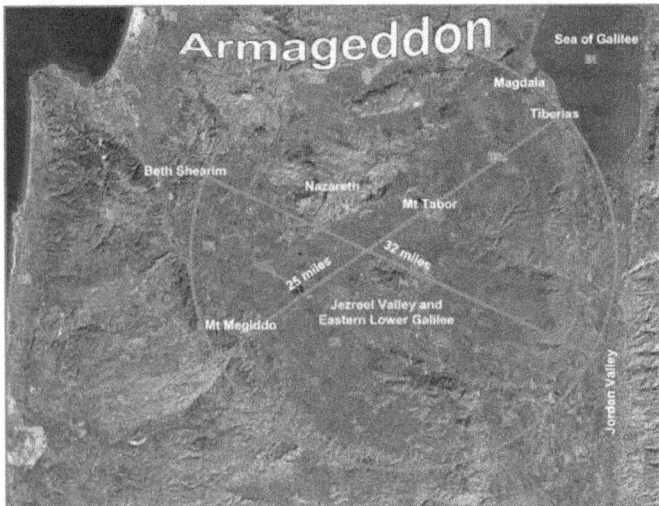

He gathered them together into the place which is called in Hebrew, "Megiddo."

Most people think of Armageddon as a fantasy or a fictional place, but it is a real archeological site in Israel. Many battles have been fought there, for it is a plain suitable to hold armies[7].

August 25 – Revelation 16:17

The seventh poured out his bowl into the air. A loud voice came out of the temple of heaven, from the throne, saying, "It is done!"

What happens at the seventh plague?

What comes out of the temple of heaven?

What does the voice say?

Why is this said?

Prayer: Father, it seems that just as Jesus said, "It is finished" at His death, so He says, "It is done!" at the death of the wicked on the Earth. You also end all the systemic wicked in the world, all the religions and governments that lie to promote themselves. Praise to You God, for giving us relief from oppression. Amen.

The seventh poured out his bowl into the air. Each plague bowl is poured in a specific place: 1) bowl poured on the earth; 2) bowl poured on the sea; 3) bowl poured on the fresh waters and streams; 4) bowl poured on the sun; 5) bowl poured on the throne of the beast; 6) bowl poured on the Euphrates; 7) bowl poured into the air. In every case, the plague's effect came from that region.

August 26 – Revelation 16:18

There were lightnings, sounds, and thunders; and there was a great earthquake, such as has not happened since there were men on the earth, so great an earthquake, and so mighty.

What happens during the seventh plague?

1.

2.

3.

4.

How great is the earthquake?

Prayer: Lord Jesus, You said there would be great tribulation and trouble, like never before, preceding Your return. You said the only reason any would survive would be because of the elect. O Lord God, save as many as possible, even to this time of terrible punishment! Amen.

There was a great earthquake, such as has not happened since there were men on the earth. The estimates for man's time on Earth range between fifty and three hundred thousand years. Regardless, this earthquake is the worst.

August 27 – Revelation 16:19

The great city was divided into three parts, and the cities of the nations fell. Babylon the great was remembered in the sight of God, to give to her the cup of the wine of the fierceness of his wrath.

What happens to the great city?

What happens to the cities of nations?

What happens to Babylon?

Prayer: Lord God, in every previous earthquake, people from unaffected areas helped those hurt by the earthquake. In this plague, everyone is affected. Have mercy, Lord God Almighty, and save these people! Amen.

The great city was divided into three parts, and the cities of the nations fell. The *Asbury Bible Commentary*[1] says the great city is Rome. *The Bible Panorama*[2] commentary says it is Babylon, as does the *IVP New Testament Commentary*[3] and *Matthew Henry's Commentary*[6]. The combination of a super earthquake, which causes all to flee out of buildings into the open, and a super hailstorm, is especially deadly. But there is no repentance.

August 28 – Revelation 16:20

Every island fled away, and the mountains were not found.

What are the other effects of the earthquake?

1.

2.

How will these things affect mankind?

Prayer: Holy Father, this worldwide earthquake has worldwide effects and death. Most of mankind lives on islands and coastlands. We need the mountains to catch the rain and water the earth. We cannot imagine this, but we cry for mercy for us and all mankind. In Jesus's Name, we pray. Amen.

Every island fled away, and the mountains were not found. Whether islands submerged or were overwhelmed by tsunamis, it doesn't matter. The only survivors will be those on ships that endure the tumultuous waves. The mountains disappearing bring to mind the Scriptures that the mountains will be made low before the King, Jesus Christ.

Isaiah 40:4 *Every valley shall be exalted, and every mountain and hill shall be made low. The uneven shall be made level, and the rough places a plain.*

Luke 3:5 *Every valley will be filled. Every mountain and hill will be brought low. The crooked will become straight, and the rough ways smooth.*

August 29 – Revelation 16:21

Great hailstones, about the weight of a talent[6] came down out of the sky on people. People blasphemed God because of the plague of the hail, for this plague is exceedingly severe.

What is the last part of the seventh plague?

How heavy were the hailstones?

What did people do?

Prayer – Father in heaven, this is the last of Your wrath. We can imagine people killed by the blows of such hail, and even by the cold of the piled-up hail. Yet mankind continues to live past this plague, for which we are grateful. We who are Your children, help us to have compassion to comfort them at that time. In Jesus's Name, we pray. Amen.

Great hailstones, about the weight of a talent – The WEB footnote below has the talent at 66 pounds[13]. The *Encyclopedia Britannica* has 75 pounds[9]. Regardless, such a hailstone is deadly.

Dividing the Talent

One Talent = 60 minas = 75 pounds = 35 kilograms

August 30 – Revelation 17:1

One of the seven angels who had the seven bowls came and spoke with me, saying, "Come here. I will show you the judgment of the great prostitute who sits on many waters."

When does this scene take place?

Where does this scene take place: in heaven or on Earth?

Who is involved in this scene?

1.

2.

Prayer: Father, You've given us Scripture, but You haven't always made it easy to understand, particularly prophecies. Help us to be careful and diligent to pick out every meaning You put into Scripture and not assign any incorrect meaning. In Jesus's Name, the Word of God, we pray. Amen.

"I will show you the judgment of the great prostitute who sits on many waters." We have seen God's woman in chapter 12, who may represent Eve, Mary, Israel, and/or the Church. Here is Satan's woman. She is shown quite differently.

August 31 – Revelation 17:2

"With whom the kings of the earth committed sexual immorality. Those who dwell in the earth were made drunken with the wine of her sexual immorality."

What is said to John? (verses 1-2)

What has the great prostitute done?

Who else is involved in her sins?

1.

2.

Does this verse give a clue about where the vision takes place? On Earth or in heaven?

Do you think sexual immorality is literal or figurative or both? Why?

Prayer: Lord God, we are espoused to one King, Jesus Christ, our Lord. Let us not stray to any ruler of the Earth, no matter how good they look or what miracles they may perform. Keep us from being deceived, we pray! Amen.

"With whom the kings of the earth committed sexual immorality." It was common in the ancient world, Roman Empire, and before for men and kings to have sex with priestesses to cement their covenant and faithfulness to their gods. This is both literal immorality, being unfaithful to their wives, and figurative, in worshiping another god besides the Almighty Creator God.

Note this immorality affects the whole world, making all drunk, unbalanced, and unable to think clearly.

September 1 – Revelation 17:3

He carried me away in the Spirit into a wilderness. I saw a woman sitting on a scarlet-colored beast, full of blasphemous names, having seven heads and ten horns.

Where is John?

What does he see?

1.

2.

What is this scarlet-colored beast?

Prayer: Holy Father, You keep giving us clues about what is going on. Now we see this woman riding a beast, which You previously revealed in Revelation 13. Help us to understand the layers of this prophecy, and how one symbol relates to the other, for it's easy to get confused. In Jesus's Name, we pray. Amen.

I saw a woman sitting on a scarlet-colored beast, full of blasphemous names, having seven heads and ten horns. In **Revelation 13:1** we saw this beast appear and be given the power and authority of Satan. Now this woman appears, controlling and directing this deceit of Satan.

Revelation 13:1 *Then I stood on the sand of the sea. I saw a beast coming up out of the sea, having ten horns and seven heads. On his horns were ten crowns, and on his heads, blasphemous names.*

The beast came from the sea, and the woman sits on many waters. They represent the same thing: many nations and ethnicities.

September 2 – Revelation 17:4

The woman was dressed in purple and scarlet, and decked with gold and precious stones and pearls, having in her hand a golden cup full of abominations and the impurities of the sexual immorality of the earth.

How does the woman appear?

1.

2.

3.

What does the cup contain?

Prayer: Lord God, not only are the political leaders using Your Name in vain blasphemies, but also the religious leaders who work in concert with them, for power and authority over people. Save us and save the world from such deceit, we pray. Amen.

The woman was dressed in purple and scarlet, and decked with gold and precious stones and pearls. It's a useful Bible study to look up purple and scarlet, gold, precious stones, and pearls and see how they are used in the Bible. I did so and learned all are associated with the Tabernacle, the Temple, and Israel, as God's bride in Ezekiel 16.

–

September 3 – Revelation 17:5

And on her forehead a name was written, "MYSTERY, BABYLON THE GREAT, THE MOTHER OF THE PROSTITUTES AND OF THE ABOMINATIONS OF THE EARTH."

What was written on the woman's forehead?

What does this mean?

What was on the foreheads of God's people in Revelation 7?

Prayer: Holy Father, let us cling to Your Spirit and not be deceived by anything in the world, whether words or miracles. Sustain us with the faith of Jesus Christ we pray. Amen

"BABYLON THE GREAT, THE MOTHER OF THE PROSTITUTES AND OF THE ABOMINATIONS OF THE EARTH." This is a title given to Babylon by God. Babylon is first a city: Babel, a rebellious city against God, led by Nimrod, then a conquering world empire under Nebuchadnezzar. It's emblematic of human rebellion against God. Satellite cities around Babylon are called "daughters." Prostitution refers to forsaking God in favor of idols.

—

September 4 – Revelation 17:6

I saw the woman drunken with the blood of the saints, and with the blood of the martyrs of Jesus. When I saw her, I wondered with great amazement[12].

(Or . . . I was amazed beyond measure (Twentieth Century New Testament), from *Twenty-Six Translations of the Bible, Volume*[3])

How did John react to Babylon?

Why did he react this way?

How does this image link to the fifth seal in Revelation 6:9-11?

Prayer: Lord God, the sin and audacity of mankind will truly be amazing, even stupefying. Help us to keep our eyes fixed on You and trust in Your justice when it looks like all is lost. In Jesus's Name, the Savior of all mankind, we pray. Amen.

Woman drunken with the blood of the saints, and with the blood of the martyrs. Here we have the abominations defined from the previous verse: God's saints killed for being Christian. This has gone on since the death of James and Stephen in Acts. This also points back to what the angel says after the third bowl plague earlier in Revelation:

Revelation 16:6 *"For they poured out the blood of saints and prophets, and you have given them blood to drink. They deserve this."*

September 5 – Revelation 17:7

The angel said to me, "Why do you wonder? I will tell you the mystery of the woman, and of the beast that carries her, which has the seven heads and the ten horns."

Who promises to reveal the mystery of the woman Babylon?

What other mystery will be revealed?

Do you think John was as puzzled by these visions as we are?

Prayer: Father, even when You reveal great mysteries of the future, we are puzzled by Your symbolism and revelation. Help us to understand, for we are but flesh. In the Name of the Word of God, Jesus the Revelator, we pray. Amen.

"The mystery of the woman, and of the beast that carries her, which has the seven heads and the ten horns." Here are three symbols in this vision or parable. The angel will explain the meaning, just as angels explained the symbols in **Daniel 7, 8, and 9.**

September 6 – Revelation 17:8

"The beast that you saw was, and is not; and is about to come up out of the abyss and to go into destruction. Those who dwell on the earth and whose names have not been written in the book of life from the foundation of the world will marvel when they see that the beast was, and is not, and yet is."

How is the beast described?

Where does the beast come from?

What will happen to the beast?

Who wonders at the beast?

Prayer: O Father, You have the power of life over death, and so does Jesus. Let us not be deceived by anyone else bringing someone back to life and urging us to worship anyone other than You. We are vulnerable to deception, but You are our strong tower. You are the Way, the Truth, and the Life. Amen.

When they behold the beast that was, and is not, and yet is. This beast existed in the past, doesn't exist now, and yet is in the world. No wonder everyone wonders about the beast. This cryptic description is short and makes us wonder what kind of miracle Satan performs. It is some great deception that fools the whole world.

September 7 – Revelation 17:9

"Here is the mind that has wisdom. The seven heads are seven mountains on which the woman sits."

Where does the woman sit?

Are these literal mountains or figurative?

What kind of mind has wisdom?

Prayer: Father, fount of all wisdom, give our minds wisdom to understand this woman Babylon. Help us so we are not deceived, but instead trained to be filled with awe at You and Your Word. In Jesus's Name, we pray. Amen.

The seven heads are seven mountains on which the woman sits. People look for cities with seven mountains or hills to fulfill the part of Babylon. These mountains may well be seven nations or kingdoms over which the woman rules. Note that the woman is used to represent a city throughout the Bible. Scripture also uses women to represent a church or religion.

September 8 – Revelation 17:10

"They are seven kings. Five have fallen, the one is, the other has not yet come. When he comes, he must continue a little while."

Are these kings concurrent or sequential?

The prophecy viewpoint is during which king?

How long will the seventh king reign ? (Hint: Check Revelation 11:2 and 13:5)

Prayer: Jesus, just as You will come to the Earth as our king, so Satan will send his king to this Earth to lead the world against You. Empower us to always follow You and never falter. Amen.

"They are seven kings. Five have fallen, the one is, the other has not yet come." The phrase "They are" refers back to the seven mountains in the previous verse. Thus the seven mountains are seven kings, and they are sequential in this prophecy. The last king is to be the beast, who in turn is ruled by the woman, who is also a symbol for a city or a church or both.

September 9 - Revelation 17:11

"The beast that was, and is not, is himself also an eighth, and is of the seven; and he goes to destruction."

The beast is the eighth of what?

How can the beast be both of the seven and the eighth?

What is the beast's final destination?

Prayer: Father, You know all the details of the future, enough to make Your prophecies to us exactly correct, and yet seemingly contradictory and irreconcilable. We see how You fulfilled the hundreds of prophecies about Jesus's first coming. We trust You to fulfill the second-coming prophecies as well. Help us to be faithful. Amen.

"Is himself also an eighth, and is of the seven." This contradictory verse has other verses like it:

Daniel 7:8 *I considered the horns, and behold, there came up among them another horn, a little one, before which three of the first horns were plucked up by the roots: and behold, in this horn were eyes like the eyes of a man, and a mouth speaking great things.*

Daniel 7:24 *As for the ten horns, ten kings will arise out of this kingdom. Another will arise after them; and he will be different from the former, and he will put down three kings.*

The ten horns are ten kings. The little horn replaces three horns, leaving seven kings, of which he is the eighth. This verse may refer to the same kings or a similar situation.

September 10 – Revelation 17:12

"The ten horns that you saw are ten kings who have received no kingdom as yet, but they receive authority as kings with the beast for one hour."

What are the ten horns?

Are these simultaneous or sequential in time?

How long do they have authority?

How do they get authority?

Prayer: Jesus, You used parables to hide Your meaning, but You explained them to Your disciples. Please explain the visions in Revelation, which are like parables with symbolic meanings to us. Amen.

But they receive authority as kings with the beast for one hour. This seems to be a classic political deal where the beast delegates power to ten subordinate kings in exchange for loyalty. This is a believable scenario. Note the time of "one hour" may not be literal, but it indicates a very short time of stability.

September 10 – Revelation 17:13

"These have one mind, and they give their power and authority to the beast."

What are these ten kings like?

What do these ten kings do?

Where does their power come from?

Prayer: Father, people love power, and we always want more. We give power to get power. Help us, Your children, not to be ensnared in this lust for power, but to give to You and our fellow human beings out of love. In Jesus's Name, we pray. Amen.

"These have one mind, and they give their power and authority to the beast." Here we have the beast's power coordinating an international alliance, which he then directs. The beast seems to have some ability to put people in power as kings.

September 12 – Revelation 17:14

"These will war against the Lamb, and the Lamb will overcome them, for he is Lord of lords, and King of kings, and those who are with him are called chosen and faithful."

What will these kings do?

What is the outcome of the war between the lamb and the beast?

Who is with the Lamb?

1.

2.

3.

Prayer: Almighty God, thank You for calling and choosing us, apart from any will or work of our own. Help us to live up to our calling and be faithful to You and Jesus Christ forever. Amen.

"These will war against the Lamb, and the Lamb will overcome them." It may seem Satan is foolish to fight against Jesus, and so he is. But his plan may be to get all of humanity to fight God. God in His justice will destroy his enemies. If Satan can get God to destroy humanity, Satan wins. But God has reserved His chosen ones who do not go Satan's way. As usual, God outsmarts Satan. See the book of Job to see this in action.

September 13 - Revelation 17:15

He said to me, "The waters which you saw, where the prostitute sits, are peoples, multitudes, nations, and languages."

Who is speaking to whom?

What is the meaning of the waters?

1.

2.

3.

4.

Prayer: Father, in addition to cloaking future events in symbols, You also provide multiple points of view and multiple time sequences. Help us to rest in You and trust in Your revelation, waiting patiently for You to reveal its meaning at the right time. In the Name of Jesus, the Revelator, we pray. Amen.

"The waters which you saw, where the prostitute sits, are peoples, multitudes, nations, and languages." God uses water to represent the various peoples of the world in all their diversity. Thus, the prostitute rules over many people, nations, and languages. This is what gives her power over the beast, for she directs the people to follow the beast.

September 14 - Revelation 17:16

"The ten horns which you saw, and the beast, these will hate the prostitute, will make her desolate, will strip her naked, will eat her flesh, and will burn her utterly with fire."

What will the kings do to Babylon?

1.

2.

3.

4.

5.

Prayer: Father, you have taught us through Jesus that as we sow, we reap. The kings got power from the woman and then used that power to destroy her. Help us to pay attention to where we sow our time, energy, and money, so that we may reap a good harvest and not an evil one. In Jesus's Name, we pray. Amen.

"These will hate the prostitute, will make her desolate, will strip her naked, will eat her flesh, and will burn her utterly with fire." A gruesome fate for this city and/or religion. Yet this is what Jesus prophesied: those that live by the sword will die by the sword. The woman killed God's saints, and now she is killed by her allies.

September 15 - Revelation 17:17

"For God has put in their hearts to do what he has in mind, to be of one mind, and to give their kingdom to the beast, until the words of God should be accomplished."

Who has put these things into the hearts of these kings?

What things were put into their hearts?

1.

2.

Why was this done?

Prayer: Father, why do we, whom You've called, ever resist Your will? Even Your bitter enemies cannot resist You, so how much less so we who love You? Help us to have one mind and Spirit with You. In Jesus's Name, we pray. Amen.

"To be of one mind, and to give their kingdom to the beast, until the words of God should be accomplished." God Himself ensures these ten are united under the beast to perform His will. What is his will? It seems to be to destroy Babylon, the city/religion/system of this world.

September 16 - Revelation 17:18

"The woman whom you saw is the great city, which reigns over the kings of the earth."

Who is the woman Babylon?

What does she do?

What city in John's day ruled over the kings of the earth?

Prayer: Father, You picture the woman as a ruling city. A city that is a capital, a leader, a dictator over the Earthly governments. Let us not look to this world but to our heavenly city and King, Jesus Christ. Amen.

"The great city, which reigns over the kings of the earth." Here we have a world government, but not for good, but evil. The city in John's day was Rome. Before that, Greece, Persia, and Babylon ruled that part of the Earth. Ultimately it goes back to Babel, the human city that sought to defy God and rule men by men.

September 17 - Revelation 18:1

After these things, I saw another angel coming down out of the sky, having great authority. The earth was illuminated with his glory.

Who did John see?

Where did the angel come from, and where was he going?

What was the angel like?

Prayer – O Father, Your very servants inspire dread and awe in us when we see them. Let us give that awe and honor to You every day as we pray, realizing that You are vaster and more powerful than anything else. In the Almighty Name of Jesus, we pray. Amen.

I saw another angel coming down out of the sky, having great authority. John sees the coming and going of many angels in the book of Revelation. God has a whole universe filled with them, and He keeps them busy. Just as He gives mankind work to do, so He does with His angels.

September 18 – Revelation 18:2

He cried with a mighty voice, saying, "Fallen, fallen is Babylon the great, and she has become a habitation of demons, a prison of every unclean spirit, and a prison of every unclean and hateful bird!"

What does the angel say?

1.

2.

3.

4.

What is the destiny of Babylon?

Prayer: Holy Father, You imprison disobedient spirits in the very place that they have created out of their malice. Your justice reigns supreme over the universe and every power, as shown in Jesus Christ our Lord. Amen.

"She has become a habitation of demons, a prison of every unclean spirit." God imprisons evil spirits in the ruins of Babylon, which they created. The idea of God imprisoning evil spirits shows up in these verses:

2 Peter 2:4 *For if God didn't spare angels when they sinned, but cast them down to hell and committed them to pits of darkness to be reserved for judgment.*

Jude 6 *Angels who didn't keep their first domain, but deserted their own dwelling place, he has kept in everlasting bonds under darkness for the judgment of the great day.*

Revelation 20:1-3 *I saw an angel coming down out of heaven, having the key of the abyss and a great chain in his hand.² He seized the dragon, the old serpent, which is the devil and Satan, who deceives the whole inhabited earth, and bound him for a thousand years,³ and cast him into the abyss, and shut it, and sealed it over him, that he should deceive the nations no more, until the thousand years were finished.*

September 19 – Revelation 18:3

"For all the nations have drunk of the wine of the wrath of her sexual immorality, the kings of the earth committed sexual immorality with her, and the merchants of the earth grew rich from the abundance of her luxury."

Why does Babylon fall?

1.

2.

3.

Prayer: Father in heaven, You are just and holy, but we often complain You don't move quickly enough against evil. These prophecies assure us that You see all the evil of the Earth, and You will repay the perpetrators in full. Help us to work steadily, advancing Your Kingdom of Your Son while we have breath. Amen.

"The merchants of the earth grew rich from the abundance of her luxury." The Bible condemns the love of money, not money itself.

1 Timothy 6:6 *For the love of money is a root of all kinds of evil. Some have been led astray from the faith in their greed, and have pierced themselves through with many sorrows.*

This verse implies the merchants used Babylon's immorality to profit themselves, at the expense of Babylon's victims. They cared only for money, not the suffering caused by Babylon.

September 20 – Revelation 18:4

I heard another voice from heaven, saying, "Come out of her, my people, that you have no participation in her sins, and that you don't receive of her plagues."

What is the warning to God's people from heaven?

Is coming out of Babylon a physical departure, a behavior change, or both?

How can the instruction to leave Babylon come after its fall and punishment?

How easy or hard will it be to leave Babylon, if you're inside her control?

Prayer: Father, You've created a complicated book. It is addressed to the seven churches and all who will listen. It portrays all church history to the present day and into the future rule of Jesus. The point of view changes from chapter to chapter and from verse to verse. Help us heed Your warnings now, to prevent or evade future disasters. In Jesus's Name, we pray. Amen.

"Come out of her, my people, that you have no participation in her sins, and that you don't receive of her plagues." Although this warning is in the middle of the chapter telling of the future judgment of Babylon, it is addressed to the church in John's day. Revelation was read aloud to seven churches in the first century. They would understand what this warning was to them at that time. Do we heed it now in our time?

September 21 – Revelation 18:5

"For her sins have reached to the sky, and God has remembered her iniquities."

Why does God judge Babylon?

What other nations or cities has God judged in the Bible?

Do you think this punishment is for one specific city or more? How much more?

Prayer: Father, help us keep the symbols in Revelation straight. Babylon represents the city of the past empire but also the city of Rome in the empire ruling in John's day. It represents the dominant world power and culture. Ultimately, it represents man's rule over man without God. Help us to be ruled by You and to obey You over men. In the Name of our King, we pray. Amen.

"For her sins have reached to the sky, and God has remembered her iniquities." The image is the sins of Babylon have piled up to heaven where God dwells. The next image is of God remembering all the past sins of mankind's government, called Babylon. God will act against sin, at His chosen time.

September 22 – Revelation 18:6

"Return to her just as she returned, and repay her double as she did, and according to her works. In the cup which she mixed, mix to her double."

How much will Babylon be punished?

What sort of punishments will Babylon receive?

How does God decide?

Prayer: Father, Your justice is evident, for You reward the saint and the sinner equally, according to our works. Help us to fear to sin, and to cleave to good works, even if they are not appreciated or noticed, for You see all. Praise to You Eternal God, Jesus Christ. Amen.

"Repay her double as she did, and according to her works." As horrific as God's plagues are, they are only according to what Babylon has done to people. Just as God gives exceedingly generously to His faithful followers, rewarding them with cities for small gains in what He gives them, so God rewards evil "generously," giving them double evil for what they have committed.

September 23 – Revelation 18:7

"However much she glorified herself, and grew wanton, so much give her of torment and mourning. For she says in her heart, 'I sit a queen, and am no widow, and will in no way see mourning.'"

How does Babylon regard herself?

What does Babylon say to herself?

1.

2.

3.

How will God punish Babylon for her attitude?

1.

2.

Prayer: O Lord our God, how dreadful it is to fall into Your hands with no grace from Jesus covering our sins! Help us to never be proud or arrogant, trusting in ourselves, in our strength and wisdom, but to wholly lean on Jesus's Name. Amen.

"For she says in her heart, 'I sit a queen, and am no widow, and will in no way see mourning.'" Here is arrogance: "I cannot fail. I cannot lose." This attitude is common in our world. Is it in us?

September 24 – Revelation 18:8

"Therefore in one day her plagues will come: death, mourning, and famine; and she will be utterly burned with fire; for the Lord God who has judged her is strong."

How quickly will Babylon's judgment come?

What is the nature of Babylon's judgment?

1.

2.

3.

4.

Who judges Babylon?

Prayer: Lord God Almighty, we often yearn for Your judgment, for the coming of Jesus, and it seems to take a long time. Yet when judgment comes with Jesus it will be swift and complete. Let us fear for the sake of humanity and show the gentle way of Jesus now. Amen.

"Therefore in one day her plagues will come: death, mourning, and famine; and she will be utterly burned with fire." Whether this is a literal day or a short period of time cannot be determined. Regardless, the proud will be humbled by death and famine and ultimately burned with fire.

September 25 – Revelation 18:9

"The kings of the earth who committed sexual immorality and lived wantonly with her will weep and wail over her, when they look at the smoke of her burning."

How will the kings of the Earth react to Babylon's fall?

1.

2.

What is the relationship the kings of the Earth had with Babylon?

1.

2.

What will prompt their mourning?

Prayer: Father, we are easily ensnared by power and money to be part and parcel with the sins of the world, oppressing the poor for our gain. You are our power and our wealth. Help us never forget this. In Jesus's Name, we pray. Amen.

"Will weep and wail over her, when they look at the smoke of her burning." Are these kings mourning over Babylon herself and the deaths of people within her? Are they mourning over their sins? No, they are mourning the loss of their power, influence, and wealth. They are no longer in charge of the world. Jesus is.

September 26 – Revelation 18:10

"Standing far away for the fear of her torment, saying, 'Woe, woe, the great city, Babylon, the strong city! For your judgment has come in one hour.'"

Where do the kings mourn?

Why do they mourn there?

What do the kings say?

How quickly does Babylon's judgment come?

Is this a literal or figurative period of time?

Prayer: Father, even the wicked fear You when they see Your judgment upon Babylon. They flee from their former ally to preserve their own lives. Help us to flee to You from the sins of this world. In Jesus's Name, we pray. Amen.

"Standing far away for the fear of her torment." Just as people flee a city being bombed, so all will flee Babylon as she burns to the ground. This is like Lot and his daughters fleeing the cities of Sodom and Gomorrah for the hills. (See **Genesis 19:30**.)

September 27 – Revelation 18:11

"The merchants of the earth weep and mourn over her, for no one buys their merchandise any more."

Who else mourns for Babylon?

Why do the merchants mourn for Babylon?

Are the merchants truly grieving for Babylon and the deaths in her or for themselves?

Prayer: Father in heaven, help us so we are not trapped into centering our lives around money and possessions. These things fail and do not satisfy our hunger for the value and love You give us. Help us to seek You first and Your righteousness, and You will supply us with all we need. In Jesus's Name, we pray. Amen.

"For no one buys their merchandise any more." Here is the source of the grief: economic ruin. The largest consuming economy in the world is wiped out suddenly. Millions of merchants are bankrupt. People who lose their possessions often grieve as they would for a loved one.

September 28 – Revelation 18:12-13

"Merchandise of gold, silver, precious stones, pearls, fine linen, purple, silk, scarlet, all expensive wood, every vessel of ivory, every vessel made of most precious wood, and of brass, and iron, and marble; and cinnamon, incense, perfume, frankincense, wine, olive oil, fine flour, wheat, sheep, horses, chariots, and people's bodies and souls."

What did Babylon buy? (Twenty-six items are listed. Pick ten.)

1.

2.

3.

4.

5.

6.

7.

8.

9.

10.

Prayer: Father, in our society we look at wealth and possessions as good things, yet here are the richest merchants of the world, and they are mourning their losses. Help us to realize our treasure is Christ Almighty, Whom we can never lose. Amen.

And people's bodies and souls. For years I took this to mean slavery would start again. Now I think it hasn't ever stopped, for all these things occur in our world today. "People's bodies" can be body parts or organs bought and sold. "Souls" refers to people's lives in official slavery, indentured servitude, or other coerced labor.

September 29 – Revelation 18:14

"The fruits which your soul lusted after have been lost to you. All things that were dainty and sumptuous have perished from you, and you will find them no more at all."

What have Babylon and the merchants lost?

List the active verbs in this verse

1.

2.

3.

4.

What can you conclude about merchants' desires from these verbs? Were they necessities or luxuries? Were their desires good or corrupt?

Prayer: Father, the easiest thing in the world is for us to lust after, and desire, some good or person intensely. We fixate on the thing or person, and nothing else matters. But only You matter, and all that we desire matters little. Help our perspective throughout the day so we remember You and Your point of view on the whole world. In Jesus's Name, we pray. Amen.

"The fruits which your soul lusted after have been lost to you." Material loss can be grievous, especially when it is your life's work. When we lose all our possessions, it can seem like the end of the world. But the loss of all things can also lead us to God.

September 30 – Revelation 18:15

"The merchants of these things, who were made rich by her, will stand far away for the fear of her torment, weeping and mourning."

Why do the merchants mourn?

Why are the merchants standing far off?

How do the merchants lament?

1.

2.

Prayer: Father, when we set our hearts on material goods, we will lament when they are lost or destroyed, for in them we placed our hopes. Let us only hope in You, our Eternal God, Who never fades or wearies but lasts forever, the foundation and the Founder of the universe. In the Name of our Creator, we pray. Amen.

"Will stand far away for the fear of her torment." All mankind flees from Babylon when God punishes the city, the society, and the system, for its sins. Review Revelation 16 to see what punishment Babylon receives.

October 1 – Revelation 18:16-17

"Saying, 'Woe, woe, the great city, she who was dressed in fine linen, purple, and scarlet, and decked with gold and precious stones and pearls!'¹⁷ For in an hour such great riches are made desolate."

How was the city of Babylon arrayed?

1.

2.

3.

4.

5.

Why do the merchants lament?

Prayer: Father, such grief is ours, if we place our trust in false gods of mankind. Whether a government, social system, or religion, if it comes from man, it will fail. Help our faith so it is wholly grounded in You, Almighty God. In the name of Jesus, the Author and Finisher of our faith, we pray. Amen.

"She who was dressed in fine linen, purple, and scarlet, and decked with gold and precious stones and pearls!" I did a word search on each of these words in the Bible and found they all pertained to the tabernacle or the temple or the garments of the priests. Thus Babylon arrays herself as the temple of God and as the priest of God, commanding all to worship. This lasts until Jesus returns and puts a stop to it.

October 2 – Revelation 18:17-18

"Every ship master, and everyone who sails anywhere, and mariners, and as many as gain their living by sea, stood far away,[18] and cried out as they looked at the smoke of her burning."

Who else mourns Babylon?

1.

2.

3.

4.

Where are these mourners?

Prayer: Father, the human world is an integrated system. Those who prosper by it would naturally mourn its destruction. Humanly, we love the familiar and hate change, even if we are poor and afflicted. But Jesus makes all things new with His second coming. Even so, come Lord Jesus! Amen.

"Every ship master, and everyone who sails anywhere, and mariners, and as many as gain their living by sea." Most commerce is conducted by the sea. It is far more important than people realize. International trade leads to prosperity worldwide—except for those afflicted and oppressed.

October 3 – Revelation 18:18-19

"Saying, 'What is like the great city?'[19] They cast dust on their heads, and cried, weeping and mourning, saying, 'Woe, woe, the great city, in which all who had their ships in the sea were made rich by reason of her great wealth!' For she is made desolate in one hour."

How do they mourn?

1.

2.

What do they say as they mourn?

Why do they mourn?

Prayer: Father, as Jesus taught us, we cannot serve God and money. Let us only serve You and accept whatever wealth or money You may give us. Let us never sell our lives to be rich in the world's goods, but only in Your love. In Jesus's Name, we pray. Amen.

"All who had their ships in the sea were made rich by reason of her great wealth!" We see a flourishing economy under Babylon. We have great consumption by the Babylon city/system. We see wealthy merchants and prosperity by the shippers, the logistics agents of the world. But what good is prosperity built by slavery and the abuse of humanity? Thus, Jesus destroys it at His coming.

October 4 – Revelation 18:20

"Rejoice over her, O heaven, you saints, apostles, and prophets; for God has judged your judgment on her."

Who is commanded to rejoice over Babylon?

1.

2.

3.

4.

Why should heaven, saints, apostles, and prophets rejoice?

Prayer: Father, the suffering on Earth is very great, and You are often accused of being indifferent. But You seek the lost, and You give the most wicked a chance to repent. Help us to remember these verses and believe You will administer justice in the end. In Jesus's Name, we pray. Amen.

"You saints, apostles, and prophets; for God has judged your judgment on her." All that befalls Babylon is what they have done to God's children. "Saints" refers to everyone God has saved. "Apostles' are those that have been sent by God. "Prophets" are God's spokesmen and spokeswomen, who speak what God tells them to say. All have been hurt, abused, tortured, and killed throughout history by those who oppose God.

October 5 – Revelation 18:21

A mighty angel took up a stone like a great millstone and cast it into the sea, saying, "Thus with violence will Babylon, the great city, be thrown down, and will be found no more at all."

What does a mighty angel do?

What does the angel say?

Do you think this happens on Earth or is it a symbolic act in heaven?

Prayer: Father, it comforts us to know violence will cease with the violent demise of man's government. O come quickly, Lord Jesus, and bring peace to this world! Amen.

"Thus with violence will Babylon, the great city, be thrown down." God gives us another picture of Babylon: they are a millstone, weighing done all humanity. Jesus will take this burden from us and throw it into the sea. This is like Pharoah's armies being destroyed in the Red Sea.

October 6 – Revelation 18:22

"The voice of harpists, minstrels, flute players, and trumpeters will be heard no more at all in you. No craftsman, of whatever craft, will be found any more at all in you. The sound of a mill will be heard no more at all in you."

What sounds cease from Babylon?

1.

2.

3.

4.

What work ceases in Babylon?

1.

2.

Prayer: Father, the end of a city, the end of a system, can be tragic. But when the whole system does evil continually, misusing even good things for evil purposes, its end can only benefit mankind. Quickly bring an end to all evil deception, Lord God! Amen.

"The voice of harpists, minstrels, flute players, and trumpeters." The angel lists all the instrumental categories: stringed instruments, vocalists, woodwinds, and brass. The good qualities of music can be misused.

October 7 – Revelation 18:23

"The light of a lamp will shine no more at all in you. The voice of the bridegroom and of the bride will be heard no more at all in you; for your merchants were the princes of the earth; for with your sorcery all the nations were deceived."

What sight ceases from Babylon?

What activity ceases from Babylon?

Why does this judgment come upon Babylon?

Prayer: Father, You eliminate light and joy from Babylon, for it only produces darkness and suffering. You will no longer permit its deceptions to mislead all nations. Bring truth and light, Jesus Christ! Amen.

"For your merchants were the princes of the earth." Here we see the merger of business and government. The businessmen were the same as the rulers of the Earth. This practice is common today and has been so throughout history.

October 8 – Revelation 18:24

"In her was found the blood of prophets and of saints, and of all who have been slain on the earth."

What is the other reason for Babylon's punishment?

Is the guilt of all murders throughout history imputed to Babylon?

Does this include the guilt of Cain for the murder of his brother Abel?

Was he part of Babylon?

Prayer: Father, beginning with Cain, men have murdered men for hurts and offenses they have perceived. Sadly, mankind institutionalized this, making murder government policy for offenses and slights against the government. Bring Your government, Jesus, of truth and justice only. People will reap what they sow, no more and no less. Amen.

"And of all who have been slain on the earth" This is a massive load of guilt—all murders ever committed are attributed to the Babylonian government system.

–

October 9 - Revelation 19:1

After these things I heard something like a loud voice of a great multitude in heaven, saying, "Hallelujah! Salvation, power, and glory belong to our God."

What does the great voice of many people in heaven say?

1.

2.

3.

4.

Prayer: Like a sigh of relief after a tremendous burden is removed, we praise You, Lord God Almighty, for removing the burden of human government and religions from the world. You have given us relief from sin and death through Jesus Christ, and now You remove all the causes of injustice. Hallelujah! Amen.

"Hallelujah! Salvation, power, and glory belong to our God." "Hallelujah" is "Praise to Jah" or the "I am." This is God's personal Name He gave Moses. Salvation comes through Jesus Christ, the Son of God and the Creator of all things. Power is given through the Holy Spirit. All glory is God's.

October 10 – Revelation 19:2

"For his judgments are true and righteous. For he has judged the great prostitute, who corrupted the earth with her sexual immorality, and he has avenged the blood of his servants at her hand."

Why do they praise God?

Why has God judged Babylon?

1.

2.

Prayer: Glorious are Your ways, O God, for all the wicked oppressors are crushed, and the oppressed and slaves are freed. Those who were slaughtered because they would not worship Satan are avenged and resurrected, praising You. Amen.

"He has avenged the blood of his servants at her hand." People often condemn the death penalty even for murderers, saying the death of the murderer does not bring the dead back to life. God's perspective is that a murderer loses the right to his or her life and that until their blood is spilled, injustice prevails. Jesus paid the penalty for all murderers, but without accepting His atoning sacrifice, the murderers' debt remains.

–

October 11 – Revelation 19:3

A second said, "Hallelujah! Her smoke goes up forever and ever."

What do the saints repeat?

What ascends forever?

Prayer: Father, practically every revelation in Your book of Revelation leads to further questions. So You have made us wonder at all things. Help us to be patient and wait for the revealing of in Jesus Christ. In His Name, Amen.

"Her smoke goes up forever and ever." One wonders how smoke can ascend forever. Does it go into outer space, obscuring the stars? Does it continue into the new heavens and new Earth? Is "forever" only an age or a long period? God does not answer these questions. Nevertheless, it remains a sign of the destruction of the wicked city of Babylon.

—

October 12 – Revelation 19:4

The twenty-four elders and the four living creatures fell down and worshiped God who sits on the throne, saying, "Amen! Hallelujah!"

Who else worships God?

1.

2.

Prayer: Father Almighty, You perpetualize the destruction of Babylon with her smoke. All will see and remember what Jesus Christ rescued us from, even as we live under His rule forever. Amen.

The twenty-four elders and the four living creatures fell down and worshiped God. These heavenly beings were introduced in chapter 4, and they are still worshipping God thousands of years later. This time they worship God for taking rulership of the Earth.

–

October 13 – Revelation 19:5

A voice came from the throne, saying, "Give praise to our God, all you his servants, you who fear him, the small and the great!"

What is commanded?

Where does the command come from?

Who is commanded to praise?

1.

2.

3.

Prayer: Ah Father, we are all small next to You, but You accept our praise anyway. What a simple command You give, and it is so easy to obey, for our hearts fully want to praise You for Your victory over sin, death, and the entire hostile world. Amen.

"All you his servants, you who fear him, the small and the great!" These are not exclusive categories of those who are commanded to praise but overlapping ones. Those who follow Jesus serve Him. Those who fear God follow Jesus. And the Father calls both small and great people to follow Him.

—

October 14 – Revelation 19:6

I heard something like the voice of a great multitude, and like the voice of many waters, and like the voice of mighty thunders, saying, "Hallelujah! For the Lord our God, the Almighty, reigns!"

Who praises next?

What do they say?

1.

2.

Prayer: Lord God, not only do all Your servants on Earth praise You but also all the millions of angels in heaven praise You at the culmination of Your plan, the salvation of mankind and the Earth from sin and death. Amen.

The voice of a great multitude, and like the voice of many waters, and like the voice of mighty thunders. No human nor group of humans has such a voice, but the voice of the heavenly beings around the throne and the millions of angels would sound like this.

–

October 15 – Revelation 19:7

"Let's rejoice and be exceedingly glad, and let's give the glory to him. For the wedding of the Lamb has come, and his wife has made herself ready."

Why do they rejoice?

1.

2.

Who do you think this great multitude is?

Prayer: Lord Jesus, You taught us Your Kingdom was like a wedding feast, and all were invited. We marvel that the angels in heaven will attend to us as we, the church, marry You, our God. Glory to You forever. Amen.

"For the wedding of the Lamb has come, and his wife has made herself ready". Who is the bride? The bride is the church, as shown in **Revelation 14**. The history of the church has been a theme of **Revelation**, from chapters **1-3** to **6-7, 10-12, 14, 19-22.**

October 16 – Revelation 19:8

And to her was granted that she should be arrayed in fine linen, clean and white: for the fine linen is the righteousness of saints.

What was granted to the bride of Christ?

What does fine linen represent?

Who is the bride of Christ?

Prayer: O holy Father, dress us now in the righteousness of Christ — pure, white, and spotless. Take away all our inclination to sin, and help us to always turn our eyes to Jesus. Amen.

For the fine linen is the righteousness of saints. Where does this righteous clothing come from? Paul has the answer:

Romans 4:5-7 *But to him who does not work but believes on Him who justifies the ungodly, his faith is accounted for righteousness,[6] just as David also describes the blessedness of the man to whom God imputes righteousness apart from works:[7] "Blessed are those whose lawless deeds are forgiven, And whose sins are covered."*

Thus, the righteousness of the saints comes from faith in Jesus Christ.

October 17 – Revelation 19:9

He said to me, "Write, 'Blessed are those who are invited to the wedding supper of the Lamb.'" He said to me, "These are true words of God."

Who receives a blessing?

Who is invited to the wedding supper of the Lamb?

Who says the blessing?

Where does the blessing come from?

Prayer: Father, You are so kind. You use Your angels as messengers carrying Your glorious words. They are like your human prophets, communicating Your words to the world. Even in speaking Your blessings, You involve Your creation. Thank You. Amen.

"'Blessed are those who are invited to the wedding supper of the Lamb.'" When I see a blessing in Scripture, I want to understand who receives the blessing. Here it is those invited to the marriage supper of the Lamb. But who are those? We know it is not the bride. The bride needs no invitation. We also know the angels will be involved. What about the rest of mankind? Jesus says in His parable of the marriage supper, all were invited, both good and evil. Some rejected the invitation, and they were destroyed. I can only conclude that all mankind then living will be invited. (See **Matthew 22:1-14**.)

October 18 – Revelation 19:10

I fell down before his feet to worship him. He said to me, "Look! Don't do it! I am a fellow bondservant with you and with your brothers who hold the testimony of Jesus. Worship God, for the testimony of Jesus is the Spirit of Prophecy."

Who falls to worship?

Who forbids him?

Who is speaking?

Who should be worshipped?

Prayer: Father, when we encounter a person full of Your Spirit, proclaiming Your word, we tend to idolize that person. How much more so would we feel in the presence of a holy angel? But all holiness and glory come from You. Let us only worship You who gives us Jesus and His testimony, the Spirit of Prophecy. Amen.

"I am a fellow bondservant with you and with your brothers who hold the testimony of Jesus." The angel in humility calls himself a fellow slave, like John and other Christians. This slavery is voluntary, where we surrender ourselves to Jesus, instead of to our sins.

—

October 19 – Revelation 19:11

I saw the heaven opened, and behold, a white horse, and he who sat on it is called Faithful and True. In righteousness he judges and makes war.

What does John see?

What is His Name?

What does He do?

1.

2.

How does He do these things?

Prayer: Lord Christ, we can't grasp how You can love us so much to die for us and then, with the same love, make war on Your enemies. Help us to understand You surpass human categories and are unique in Yourself, in Your love and majesty. Amen.

He who sat on it is called Faithful and True. In righteousness he judges and makes war. Jesus is Faithful to His covenants, to His people, and to His character. He cannot abide murderers and thieves in His kingdom, and He makes war on them.

—

October 20 – Revelation 19:12

His eyes were as a flame of fire, and on his head were many crowns; and he had a name written, that no man knew, but he himself.

How does Jesus appear?

1.

2.

What is written?

Prayer: Lord Christ, we met You in Revelation 1 with Your blazing eyes of fire. Now all the world meets You as You are. Help everyone to learn You are God, and there is no other. Amen.

On his head are many crowns. Crowns indicate kingship. Jesus is king over many: all the Earth, all of heaven, all of the angels. The whole universe is His realm, and not just at this time, but for all time.

–

October 21 – Revelation 19:13

He is clothed in a garment sprinkled with blood. His name is called "The Word of God."

How is Jesus dressed?

What is the significance of His clothing?

What is His Name?

Prayer: Holy Father, from the beginning, with Adam and Eve, You decreed that sin must be paid in blood. Thus the death penalty came upon us all since then. Jesus took the full penalty upon Himself, paying for our sins and freeing us from death. Yet those who resist Him still must pay in their blood. Help us understand Your wisdom. In Jesus's Name, we pray. Amen.

He is dressed in a robe sprinkled/dipped in blood. Two different translations give two different connotations and interpretations to this verse. "Sprinkled" brings to mind:

Isaiah 52:14-15 *As many were astonied at thee; his visage was so marred more than any man, and his form more than the sons of men:*[15] *So shall he sprinkle many nations; the kings shall shut their mouths at him: for that which had not been told them shall they see; and that which they had not heard shall they consider.* (KJV)

This connotes Jesus's shed blood sprinkling the nations and cleansing them from sin.

The Amplified translation of **Revelation 19:13**: *He is dressed in a robe dipped in blood, and His name is called The Word of God .*

This translation brings this verse to mind:

Isaiah 63:1-3 *"Who is this who comes from Edom, with dyed garments from Bozrah? Who is this who is glorious in his clothing, marching in the greatness of his strength?*

"It is I who speak in righteousness, mighty to save."[2] *Why is your clothing red, and your garments like him who treads in the wine vat?"*[3] *"I have trodden the wine press alone. Of the peoples, no one was with me. Yes, I trod them in my anger and trampled them in my wrath. Their lifeblood is sprinkled on my garments, and I have stained all my clothing."*

This connotes Jesus treading out the winepress of His wrath upon the wicked, and His clothing is stained with their blood.

October 22 – Revelation 19:14

The armies which are in heaven followed him on white horses, clothed in white, pure, fine linen.

Who follows Jesus?

How do they travel?

How are they dressed?

Prayer: Lord God Almighty, everything in creation teaches us about You. Here we have heavenly horses. In this world, we admire horses for their strength and beauty. We have used horses for our wars. It is just You use them in Your war to end all wars. Praise to You forever. Amen.

The armies which are in heaven followed Him. Who are these armies? The first thought is of the angels in heaven, who are also called the "host of heaven" or the "army of heaven." But another meaning can be the glorified saints of God riding horses in His army as He defeats the evil of the Earth. Remember this from earlier in Revelation:

Revelation 14:4 *These are those who were not defiled with women, for they are virgins. These are those who follow the Lamb wherever he goes. These were redeemed by Jesus from among men, the first fruits to God and to the Lamb.*

October 23 – Revelation 19:15

Out of his mouth proceeds a sharp, double-edged sword, that with it he should strike the nations. He will rule them with an iron rod. He treads the wine press of the fierceness of the wrath of God, the Almighty.

What comes from the mouth of the Lamb?

How does He use His sword?

How will Jesus rule?

How is God's wrath described?

Prayer: Ah, Eternal Father in heaven, what can mankind do against You? You are indomitable, and You conquer all the Earth through Jesus Christ. His love comes first to all who repent and believe, and then to the wicked comes His fierce anger. Let us fear and worship You today! Amen.

He treads the wine press of the fierceness of the wrath of God, the Almighty. Again, the wicked are compared to grapes (See Revelation 14.) being squeezed in a winepress. Only this is far more personal, with God Himself, Jesus Christ, treading the grapes, that is, crushing the wicked beneath Him.

October 24 – Revelation 19:16

He has on his garment and on his thigh a name written, "KING OF KINGS, AND LORD OF LORDS."

What is written on Jesus's garment and thigh?

Who are the kings and lords under Jesus's rule?

Is there anything not under Jesus's rule?

Prayer: Father, perhaps the most unbelievable aspect of Jesus's second coming is that Your humble servants, we weak and fallible followers of Jesus, will rule with Him in Your Kingdom. Help us to be faithful until the end, with this glorious future in front of us. Amen.

"KING OF KINGS, AND LORD OF LORDS." I looked for Jesus's own words about His followers ruling with Him: **Matthew 5:5** *Blessed are the gentle, for they shall inherit the earth.*

Peter's question: **Matthew 19:27-28** *Then Peter answered, "Behold, we have left everything and followed you. What then will we have?* [28] *Jesus said to them, "Most certainly I tell you that you who have followed me, in the regeneration when the Son of Man will sit on the throne of his glory, you also will sit on twelve thrones, judging the twelve tribes of Israel."*

–

October 25 – Revelation 19:17

I saw an angel standing in the sun. He cried with a loud voice, saying to all the birds that fly in the sky, "Come! Be gathered together to the great supper of the great God."

Where is an angel standing?

What does he say?

Who is invited to the great supper of the great God?

Prayer: Almighty God, You have all power over heaven and Earth. It is nothing for You to gather all the birds of the air to the wedding supper of the Lamb. Let us remember this when our problems seem overwhelming. Amen.

"Come! Be gathered together to the great supper of the great God." In a surprise twist, the birds are at God's wedding supper. Oddly, this has been done before at weddings when doves are released. But these are not doves. We will find out what kind of birds these are tomorrow.

October 26 – Revelation 19:18

"That you may eat the flesh of kings, the flesh of captains, the flesh of mighty men, and the flesh of horses and of those who sit on them, and the flesh of all men, both free and slave, small and great."

What do the birds of the air eat?

1.

2.

3.

4.

5.

6.

What kind of birds are these?

Prayer: O Lord, my God, Your enemies are not buried, but instead eaten by the birds of the air, removing their memory from the Earth. Lord Jesus, how dreadful it is to be Your enemy. Help me to always be Your friend, Eternal God. Amen.

"And the flesh of all men, both free and slave, small and great." These carrion eaters clean up after the battle, even while the wedding supper of the Lamb and the Bride is underway. Thus, the most joyful event in history is tinged with the death of the wicked who opposed Jesus's rule.

October 27 - Revelation 19:19

I saw the beast, and the kings of the earth, and their armies, gathered together to make war against him who sat on the horse, and against his army.

Who gathered to war against Jesus and His army?

1.

2.

3.

Where did they gather? (See Revelation 16:16.)

Prayer: Father, You don't think as we do, so the Bible is not written as we expect. Help us to study it carefully, thoughtfully, and prayerfully so we can understand it as You intend. In Jesus's Name, we pray. Amen.

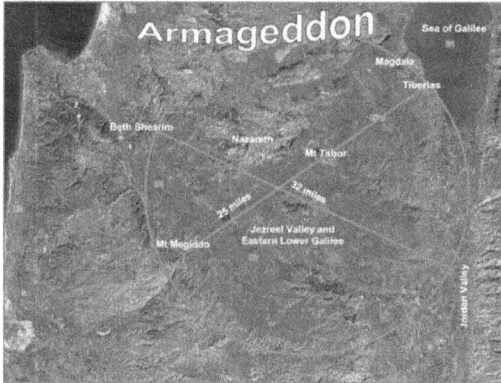

I saw the beast, and the kings of the earth, and their armies, gathered together to make war. This is similar to **Revelation 16:16** *He gathered them together into the place which is called in Hebrew, "Megiddo."* To summarize verses 17-20, the seventh plague is then poured out, followed by a worldwide earthquake and a hailstorm of seventy-pound hailstones. That chapter described the last seven plagues. This chapter describes the marriage of the Lamb and His defeat of the beast and his armies.

October 28 – Revelation 19:20

The beast was taken, and with him the false prophet who worked the signs in his sight, with which he deceived those who had received the mark of the beast and those who worshiped his image. These two were thrown alive into the lake of fire that burns with sulfur.

Who was taken alive?

1.

2.

What happened to these two?

Prayer: Father, we have many questions and debates about the lake of fire, but let us accept that is the fate of the incorrigible. Let us be pliable, moldable by Your hands into the image of Jesus Christ. In His Name, Amen.

These two were thrown alive into the lake of fire that burns with sulfur. This is the first mention of the phrase "lake of fire." Taken literally, we can imagine it as a volcanic caldera filled with lava. Given that a worldwide earthquake just occurred, it would be logical that volcanoes would appear. Since the beast and the false prophet were on Earth, the lake of fire may be on Earth as well.

October 29 – Revelation 19:21

The rest were killed with the sword of him who sat on the horse, the sword which came out of his mouth. So all the birds were filled with their flesh.

What happened to the armies?

How were they killed?

Then what happened after their deaths?

Prayer: Lord God, help us remember we are only alive because the Word of God sustains us. At Your word, we exist, and at Your word, we can perish. In Jesus's Name, we pray. Amen.

The sword which came out of his mouth. This strange image of a sword coming from the Son of Man's mouth is explained by Paul:

Ephesians 6:17 *And take the helmet of salvation, and the sword of the Spirit, which is the word of God.*

Hebrews also testifies to this explanation of the image:

Hebrews 4:12 *For the word of God is living and active, and sharper than any two-edged sword, piercing even to the dividing of soul and spirit, of both joints and marrow, and is able to discern the thoughts and intentions of the heart.*

–

October 30 - Revelation 20:1

I saw an angel coming down out of heaven, having the key of the abyss and a great chain in his hand.

Who comes down from heaven?

What does he hold?

Where is he going?

Prayer: Father, You show us many scenes from heaven and Earth that we would never know or imagine. Help us understand what this means and how we should live and behave in the light of Jesus's revelation to us. Amen.

Having the key of the abyss. This is the second time the abyss is mentioned:

Revelation 9:1-2 *The fifth angel sounded, and I saw a star from the sky which had fallen to the earth. The key to the pit of the abyss was given to him.[2] He opened the pit of the abyss, and smoke went up out of the pit, like the smoke from a burning furnace.*

The simplest explanation is this is the same pit from which the smoke and locusts come.

October 31 – Revelation 20:2

He seized the dragon, the old serpent, which is the devil and Satan, who deceives the whole inhabited earth, and bound him for a thousand years.

What happens to Satan after Jesus's return?

Who does this act?

How long is Satan bound?

Prayer: Father, we praise You that finally Satan is bound away, unable to tempt and lie to humanity. We are grateful You will give us this respite while Your Son Jesus rules as King on Earth. Speed this day, holy God! Amen.

I saw an angel coming down out of heaven, having the key of the abyss and a great chain. God delegates this job to an angel, showing that Satan is not the most powerful angel, let alone an equal to God.

November 1 – Revelation 20:3

And cast him into the abyss, and shut it, and sealed it over him, that he should deceive the nations no more, until the thousand years were finished. After this, he must be freed for a short time.

Where is Satan during the thousand years?

Why is he bound here?

What happens after a thousand years?

Prayer: Father, here we have the true start of the new age, one without Satan to deceive. You've allowed Satan to deceive to test the hearts of men and angels. Until this day comes, help us pass the test and not be deceived by Satan, but to instead hold fast to Your word. In the Name of the Word of God, we pray. Amen.

And cast him into the abyss, and shut it, and sealed it over him, that he should deceive the nations no more. God places him in an "abyss" where he cannot escape, and he is chained as well. This isolation prevents Satan from deceiving. The power of the big lie is what he uses, and both angels and people have fallen to it.

November 2 – Revelation 20:4

I saw thrones, and they sat on them, and judgment was given to them. I saw the souls of those who had been beheaded for the testimony of Jesus, and for the word of God, and such as didn't worship the beast nor his image, and didn't receive the mark on their forehead and on their hand. They lived and reigned with Christ for a thousand years.

Thrones and judgment are awarded to whom?

1.

2.

3.

4.

How long did they reign with Christ?

Prayer: Jesus Christ, You reward Your followers all out of proportion to what we do. All You ask is for us to be faithful to You even to death, and You give rulership over the Earth, even over the very countries that put Your people to death. Glory to You in the highest and, on Earth, peace among Your saints. Amen.

They lived and reigned with Christ for a thousand years. These one thousand years and the time of Satan's imprisonment are assumed to be the same. This period is what gives us the term "'millennium" which means "one thousand years."

–

November 3 – Revelation 20:5

The rest of the dead didn't live until the thousand years were finished. This is the first resurrection.

When are the rest of the dead resurrected?

What is this group of ruling saints called?

Prayer: Father, all humanity will be resurrected, but those in the first resurrection have the special blessing of ruling with Jesus. Help us who profess You to live up to this future now, showing Your love today. In Jesus's Name, we pray. Amen.

This is the first resurrection. Jesus refers to these two resurrections:

John 5:28-30 *Don't marvel at this, for the hour comes in which all who are in the tombs will hear his voice,*[29] *and will come out; those who have done good, to the resurrection of life; and those who have done evil, to the resurrection of judgment.*[30] *I can of myself do nothing. As I hear, I judge, and my judgment is righteous; because I don't seek my own will, but the will of my Father who sent me.*

Paul states this in Acts:

Acts 24:14-15 *But this I confess to you, that after the Way, which they call a sect, so I serve the God of our fathers, believing all things which are according to the law, and which are written in the prophets;*[15] *having hope toward God, which these also themselves look for, that there will be a resurrection of the dead, both of the just and unjust.*

–

November 4 – Revelation 20:6

Blessed and holy is he who has part in the first resurrection. Over these, the second death has no power, but they will be priests of God and of Christ, and will reign with him one thousand years.

Who is this blessing for?

What are the features of this blessing?

1.

2.

3.

Prayer: Father, it's not enough that we rule over the Earth with Jesus. You also make us priests, mediating between humanity and God. Just as Jesus mediates for us now, we will mediate for mankind throughout Your rule on Earth. Help us to love our brothers and sisters as You do. In Jesus's Name, we pray. Amen.

They will be priests of God and of Christ, and will reign with him one thousand years. Priests had roles as teachers and judges, as well as interceding with God on behalf of the people. All these responsibilities belong to those in the first resurrection.

November 5 – Revelation 20:7

And after the thousand years, Satan will be released from his prison,

What happens after the thousand-year rule of Christ?

Why does God do this?

What will be the effect on the world?

Prayer: Father, we must face Satan every day in our temptations and trials. Help us gain victory today, through Jesus Christ, our Lord. Amen.

Satan will be released from his prison. This seems to be a period of probation for Satan. It will also be a time of testing and trial for all those born during Jesus's reign who have never been tempted by Satan.

November 6 – Revelation 20:8

And he will come out to deceive the nations which are in the four corners of the earth, Gog and Magog, to gather them together to the war; the number of whom is as the sand of the sea.

What shall Satan do?

Whom shall Satan deceive?

What shall he cause them to do?

Prayer: Father, this mass deception is what is happening today. It's what happened with Adam and Eve, even in Your Presence, Jesus Christ. Help us, God Almighty, to cleave to You and Your word so we won't be deceived now or in the future. Amen.

And he will come out to deceive the nations which are in the four corners of the earth, Gog and Magog. Lying and deception are what Satan does. A "devil" is a deceiver. Gog and Magog seem to be somewhat generic terms to refer to nations. This may be the event prophesied in **Ezekiel 38:1-23** and **39:1-20**.

November 7 – Revelation 20:9

They went up over the width of the earth, and surrounded the camp of the saints, and the beloved city. Fire came down out of heaven from God and devoured them.

Where does the army come from?

Where does the army go to?

What is the beloved city?

How does God respond to the attack by Satan and his army?

Prayer: Father, Satan is persistent in attacking You and Your creation. He rebelled against You and attacked Adam and Eve. He attacked Israel throughout its history. He attacked Jesus. In the end time, he will seek to invade heaven again. And after his imprisonment for a thousand years, he attacks Your city and people. Help us to stand firm against his attacks now and not quail with fear but to call upon You for help. In Jesus's Name, we pray. Amen.

And surrounded the camp of the saints, and the beloved city. Jerusalem is the first city that comes to mind as beloved of God. We can find proof here:

Psalm 87:1-3 *His foundation is in the holy mountains.² Yahweh loves the gates of Zion more than all the dwellings of Jacob.³ Glorious things are spoken about you, city of God. Selah.*

The use of fire from heaven to defend God's saints occurs for Elijah in **2 Kings 1:9-15**. Then we see it again in **Revelation 11:5** where God's two witnesses can call down fire from heaven on those who seek to harm them.

November 8 – Revelation 20:10

The devil who deceived them was thrown into the lake of fire and sulfur, where the beast and the false prophet are also. They will be tormented day and night forever and ever.

What happens to Satan?

Who else was thrown into this lake of fire?

1.

2.

Prayer: We love You, Father, and we will never rebel against You nor betray You. We are weak, but You are faithful to sustain us when we're tempted. Help us today to resist the temptation to seek our way rather than Your way. In the Name of the Way, Jesus Christ, Amen.

Where the beast and the false prophet are also. These two were thrown in the lake of fire in **Revelation 19:20**. The verb "are" is implied. The New International, Amplified[13], and the Zondervan Greek Interlinear[16] have "were," referring back to the previous chapter.

November 9 - Revelation 20:11

I saw a great white throne, and him who sat on it, from whose face the earth and the heaven fled away. There was found no place for them.

What happens after Satan's final punishment?

Where does this throne appear?

Who is on the throne?

Prayer: Lord God Almighty, what can we say to You? You will judge us for all our actions and words. Yet, amazingly, it is Jesus Christ Who died for us and Who is also our living Advocate and Judge and Rewarder of our faith. Help us hold on to Him to the end. In the Name of the Way, we pray. Amen.

And him who sat on it, from whose face the earth and the heaven fled away. Traditionally this final judgment is pictured in heaven, yet both heaven and Earth flee from God. We simply don't know where this happens. But we know Jesus Christ is the Judge of all mankind.

John 5:22 *For the Father judges no one, but he has given all judgment to the Son.*

2 Corinthians 5:10 *For we must all be revealed before the judgment seat of Christ that each one may receive the things in the body according to what he has done, whether good or bad.*

November 10 – Revelation 20:12

I saw the dead, the great and the small, standing before the throne, and they opened books. Another book was opened, which is the book of life. The dead were judged out of the things which were written in the books, according to their works.

What happens after death for the non-Christian?

Where are the Christians?

How are the dead judged?

1.

2.

Prayer: Holy Father, although we fall far short of the perfection of Christ, we trust in Christ to make us right with You and to present us holy and clean at His judgment through His blood shed for us. In Him we have faith. Amen.

The dead were judged out of the things which were written in the books, according to their works. The word "books" here in Greek is "*biblia*," from which we get our word "Bible."[16]

November 11 - Revelation 20:13

The sea gave up the dead who were in it. Death and Hades gave up the dead who were in them. They were judged, each one according to his works.

Where did the dead come from?

1.

2.

3.

How were they judged?

Who is not in this resurrection?

Prayer: O Father, stir people today to respond to Jesus and to change their works to conform to Jesus Christ, so that they may live in the day of judgment. Amen.

They were judged, each one according to his works. This is according to God's teaching for 3,000 years. Psalms teach this:

Psalm 62:12 *Also to you, Lord, belongs loving kindness, for you reward every man according to his work.*

The book of Proverbs teaches this:

Proverbs 24:1 *If you say, "Behold, we didn't know this," doesn't he who weighs the hearts consider it? He who keeps your soul, doesn't he know it? Shall he not render to every man according to his work?*

Paul teaches this:

Romans 2:5-6 *But according to your hardness and unrepentant heart you are treasuring up for yourself wrath in the day of wrath, revelation, and of the righteous judgment of God;[6] who "will pay back to everyone according to their works: to those who by perseverance in well-doing seek for glory, honor, and incorruptibility, eternal life."*

November 12 – Revelation 20:14

Death and Hades were thrown into the lake of fire. This is the second death, the lake of fire.

What happens to death?

What happens to hades or the grave?

What else is the lake of fire called?

Prayer: Father, we praise You that You will destroy death and the grave. No more will they plague humanity, but all will live forever, as You intended from the beginning. We praise You in the Name of the Lord of life, the Resurrection, Jesus Christ. Amen.

Death and Hades were thrown into the lake of fire. This fulfills the prophecy:

Isaiah 25:8 *He has swallowed up death forever! The Lord Yahweh will wipe away tears from off all faces. He will take the reproach of his people away from off all the earth, for Yahweh has spoken it.*

November 13 – Revelation 20:15

If anyone was not found written in the book of life, he was cast into the lake of fire.

Who is cast into the lake of fire?

When does one's name enter the Book of Life?

How does one's name enter the Book of Life?

Prayer: Father, I pray that every reader may believe Your words and enter into the Book of Life and live forever. In the Name of Life, I pray. Amen.

If anyone was not found written in the book of life. The appendix at the back of this devotional contains the Scriptures referencing it. It is too detailed to cover in depth here.

Summarizing those Scriptures, we are written into the book before we are born. The Book of Life is written at the foundation of the world. Our body is described in it. Our whole life is contained there. All our tears and wanderings are recorded within it. The Lord Jesus can blot out names from the book. God blots out the names of those who sin against Him. Christians' names are written in the book.

November 14 - Revelation 21:1

I saw a new heaven and a new earth: for the first heaven and the first earth have passed away, and the sea is no more.

How would the Earth be different without a sea?

What happens to people during this recreation of the heavens and Earth?

What happens to the lake of fire?

Prayer: Holy Father, You take away all our fears, worries, and doubts. There is no more death. We have a permanent home in You. You make massive changes throughout the universe, but we have no fear, for we trust in You. In the name of our King Jesus, we pray. Amen.

I saw a new heaven and a new earth. Here is the point of the whole Bible. God makes a paradise or garden for mankind to dwell with Him. This is a garden city of unfathomable size, with God living in it with mankind.

November 15 – Revelation 21:2

I saw the holy city, New Jerusalem, coming down out of heaven from God, prepared like a bride adorned for her husband.

What is the first thing that appears on the new Earth?

Where does the city come from?

How does the new Jerusalem appear?

Prayer: Lord God Almighty, this is so far outside our imagination that we can't tell what is true and what might be symbolic. Either way, we trust You to exceed our wildest dreams of reality with Your new reality. Remaking reality is not as we usually think of prophecy, yet You say so. Help us to patiently wait for You to reveal the meaning of it all. In the Name of the Revelator, Jesus, we pray. Amen.

Coming down out of heaven from God, prepared like a bride adorned for her husband. Here is a clear simile: new Jerusalem is prepared like an adorned bride for her husband. How? Jesus is the husband, and He has claimed the Church as His Bride. The marriage was announced in chapter 19 along with the marriage supper. So Jesus and the Church have been married since then, all through the millennium, second resurrection, and white throne judgment. But the city isn't the bride, but is like the bride in its adornment. My conclusion is it is the permanent dwelling place for God and man, Jesus and the Bride, for eternity, in the new heavens and the new earth.

November 16 – Revelation 21:3

I heard a loud voice out of heaven saying, "Behold, God's dwelling is with people, and he will dwell with them, and they will be his people, and God himself will be with them as their God."

What is said from heaven in this verse?

1.

2.

3.

Where does this imply mankind is at this time?

Prayer: Father, since our ultimate destiny is to dwell with You through eternity, help us to love You more right now. Help us to long to spend more time with You, with Jesus Christ, abiding with You today. In the Name of the Bridegroom, we pray. Amen.

God's dwelling is with people, and he will dwell with them, and they will be his people. Consider how indomitable and relentless God is. God began to dwell with man, male and female, in the beginning, but we rejected Him and chose sin. He came to the Earth to buy us back from sin and death, and He paid the penalty in His blood so He could make this happen. Everything else in history is inconsequential.

November 17 – Revelation 21:4

"He will wipe away every tear from their eyes. Death will be no more; neither will there be mourning, nor crying, nor pain, any more. The first things have passed away."

What will God do?

What will cease to exist?

1.

2.

3.

4.

Prayer: Lord God, we're overwhelmed by Your tender love. As a mother caresses her baby and comforts it when it cries, so You will hold us in Your arms and comfort away all our past sorrows and pains until none are left. Glory to You forever, O Lord of love! Amen.

Death will be no more; neither will there be mourning, nor crying, nor pain. This is an inconceivable level of change. All of life's ecosystem revolves around death. Perhaps this will only be the end of the death of people. That alone is staggering, too. That implies there will be no more sin by any person, ever including those alive and glorified and those who may be created or born in the future.

—

November 18 - Revelation 21:5

He who sits on the throne said, "Behold, I am making all things new." He said, "Write, for these words of God are faithful and true."

What does God speak from His throne?

Why does God add "these words of God are faithful and true"?

Prayer: Father, You give us hope. We have hope in You and Jesus Christ that you will wipe away all sorrow, pain, and death from the world forever. We grow impatient with the suffering and evil all around us, but help us to keep our eyes on You. Amen.

Behold, I am making all things new. The scope of the word "all" can lead us to unimaginable changes. All scientific laws are new. All the universe is new, including all the stars and galaxies. Every person who has ever lived is new in their heart and mind.

—

November 19 – Revelation 21:6

He said to me, "I am the Alpha and the Omega, the Beginning and the End. I will give freely to him who is thirsty from the spring of the water of life."

Who names Himself "the Alpha and the Omega"?

Who has said He will give of the water of life freely?

What will life be like knowing we cannot die?

Prayer: Father, in this life we die a little every day, growing closer to our death. Yet in the world to come we will grow ever closer to You, and death will become a distant memory. Speed this day, Lord Jesus! In the name of the Alpha and the Omega, we pray. Amen.

"I will give freely to him who is thirsty from the spring of the water of life." This phrase calls to mind Jesus's words to the woman at the well:

John 4:10, 13-14 *Jesus answered her, "If you knew the gift of God, and who it is who says to you, 'Give me a drink,' you would have asked him, and he would have given you living water."[13] Jesus answered her, "Everyone who drinks of this water will thirst again,[14] but whoever drinks of the water that I will give him will never thirst again; but the water that I will give him will become in him a well of water springing up to eternal life."*

–

November 20 – Revelation 21:7

He who overcomes, I will give him these things. I will be his God, and he will be my son.

Who will receive the gifts of God?

What else does God say about overcomers?

1.

2.

Prayer: O Lord God, You give us all things. You call us and give Your Son for us and Your Spirit to help us overcome, all so that You may make us members of Your family. We thank You, in Jesus's Name. Amen

I will be his God, and he will be my son. Adam and all mankind are God's sons by creation. Christians are His sons and daughters through the new birth into His kingdom.

John 3:3, 5-8 *Jesus answered him, "Most certainly, I tell you, unless one is born anew, he can't see God's Kingdom."⁵ Jesus answered, "Most certainly I tell you, unless one is born of water and spirit, he can't enter into God's Kingdom.⁶ That which is born of the flesh is flesh. That which is born of the Spirit is spirit.⁷ Don't marvel that I said to you, 'You must be born anew.'⁸ The wind blows where it wants to, and you hear its sound, but don't know where it comes from and where it is going. So is everyone who is born of the Spirit."*

–

November 21 – Revelation 21:8

But for the cowardly, unbelieving, sinners, abominable, murderers, sexually immoral, sorcerers , idolaters, and all liars, their part is in the lake that burns with fire and sulfur, which is the second death."

Who is mentioned as not being in the new heavens and the new earth?

1.

2.

3.

4.

5.

6.

7.

8.

9.

Where will these people be in the future?

Prayer: Holy Father, Your revelation contains many wonderful promises but also severe warnings about what we must not be. Help us avoid all these sins and stay faithful to You, forever. In Jesus's Name, we pray. Amen

Their part is in the lake that burns with fire and sulfur, which is the second death. God contrasts the future of His followers with those who reject him and choose their lifestyle.

November 22 – Revelation 21:9

One of the seven angels who had the seven bowls, who were loaded with the seven last plagues came, and he spoke with me, saying, "Come here. I will show you the wife, the Lamb's bride."

Who speaks with John?

What does he show John?

Prayer: Lord and King, help us to live with You as intimately as husband and wife, and also as respectfully as King and subject. The tension of these two is impossible for humans but possible with You. Help us do the impossible for You. In Jesus's Name, we pray. Amen.

"Come here. I will show you the wife, the Lamb's bride." Thus, the new Jerusalem is portrayed as the Bride of Christ, the Church. Is this a simile, a metaphor, or literal? I think God combines similes like "bride" and "city" to better depict a complex subject outside our experience. The church will have a supremely intimate relationship with Christ. We are like a bride. The church will also live with God in the new heavens and new earth capital, which will be the new Jerusalem. We'll be the population of that city.

November 23 – Revelation 21:10

He carried me away in the Spirit to a great and high mountain, and showed me the holy city, Jerusalem, coming down out of heaven from God.

Where did John go to see new Jerusalem?

From where does new Jerusalem come?

Where is the new Jerusalem placed?

Prayer: Father, just as in Eden, when You dwelt with Adam and Eve, so You will dwell with men in the combined new heavens and new Earth. Help us to press forward now in our lives to that day and convey our excitement and eagerness to live with You to all we meet. In Jesus's Name, we pray. Amen.

The holy city, Jerusalem, coming down out of heaven from God. The new Jerusalem comes from heaven to Earth. It is made by God in heaven, presumably part of the new heavens during the great recreation of the universe. Jesus is its Maker and Builder, as a husband in Judea would build a home for his bride.

November 24 – Revelation 21:11

Having the glory of God. Her light was like a most precious stone, as if it were a jasper stone, clear as crystal.

What is the light of the new Jerusalem like?

Where does this light come from?

Why does it have the glory of God?

Prayer: Holy Father, this is hard to believe: that You dwell with us, and Your glory is reflected in us. Let us not obscure Your glory through our own will and desires but express it fully in our lives. Help us be as transparent as glass or diamond to show You to all we meet. Amen.

Her light was like a most precious stone, as if it were a jasper stone, clear as crystal. Imagine an illuminated diamond, radiating rainbows from each facet. Such is the light of the new Jerusalem. God gives us a glimpse of His throne in heaven in Revelation 4. This is His new throne on Earth.

November 25 – Revelation 21:12

Having a great and high wall; having twelve gates, and at the gates twelve angels; and names written on them, which are the names of the twelve tribes of the children of Israel.

What is the wall of new Jerusalem like?

How many gates does new Jerusalem have?

What are the names of the gates?

Who is at each gate?

Prayer: Lord God, You are completely moving Your government, Your court, to the Earth. Your angels will dwell at the gates of new Jerusalem and go in and out of it. We will dwell with You forever. Help us to keep this vision in our mind as we live and work in this world, knowing You will transform it. Amen.

Having a great and high wall; having twelve gates. The city is in the pattern of the temple but greater. There were three gates into the temple in **Ezekiel 40-45**, two of which were used. New Jerusalem will have twelve gates, each with an angel. This is like the Holy of Holies, with two cherubim, and also like the garden of Eden. But it will be far greater than either of those.

November 26 – Revelation 21:13

On the east were three gates; and on the north three gates; and on the south three gates; and on the west three gates.

How are the gates placed?

How is the city oriented?

What is the shape of the city? It's not explicitly stated here, but take your best guess.

Prayer: Lord God Almighty, You had a plan for mankind from the beginning. We started in Your presence, and we will forever be in Your presence. Help us to live now in Your presence every day, delight in You, and give our joy to all we meet. In Jesus's Name, we pray. Amen.

And on the west three gates. Unlike the temple, new Jerusalem has gates to the west. The placement of the gates indicates anyone may enter from any direction to meet God. Remember, at this time mankind will be without sin forever, and there will be no restriction on access to God.

November 27 – Revelation 21:14

The wall of the city had twelve foundations, and on them twelve names of the twelve apostles of the Lamb.

How many foundations did the wall have?

What was written on the foundations?

Why was this done?

Prayer: O Father, You have promised us an eternal inheritance in Jesus Christ and here we see the apostles permanently inscribed on the foundations of the holy city. They put their faith in You when You were in the form of a man. Help us to put our faith in You even when we can't see You. In the Name of the Lamb, we pray. Amen

The wall of the city had twelve foundations. Like a picture frame, the wall encloses the new Jerusalem. We may think of the foundations as separate layers beneath the wall. This verse is similar to:

Ephesians 2:19-21 *So then you are no longer strangers and foreigners, but you are fellow citizens with the saints and of the household of God,[20] being built on the foundation of the apostles and prophets, Christ Jesus himself being the chief cornerstone;[21] in whom the whole building, fitted together, grows into a holy temple in the Lord.*

November 28 – Revelation 21:15

He who spoke with me had for a measure a golden reed to measure the city, its gates, and its walls.

Who was with John, showing him the city?

What did he do to the city?

How did he measure the city?

Prayer: Father, we can't grasp how an angel with a simple measuring stick can measure Your gigantic new Jerusalem. Let us be humble before You and realize we are far less than Your angels in heaven in terms of strength and speed. You alone, Jesus Christ, are our strength. Amen.

He who spoke with me had for a measure a golden reed to measure the city. As far as we can tell, this is still one of the angels who carried a last plague. This verse parallels the one in Ezekiel:

Ezekiel 40:2-3, 5 *In the visions of God he brought me into the land of Israel, and set me down on a very high mountain, on which was something like the frame of a city to the south.³ He brought me there; and, behold, there was a man, whose appearance was like the appearance of bronze, with a line of flax in his hand, and a measuring reed; and he stood in the gate. …⁵ Behold, there was a wall on the outside of the house all around, and in the man's hand a measuring reed six cubits long, of a cubit and a hand width each. So he measured the thickness of the building, one reed; and the height, one reed.*

November 29 – Revelation 21:16

The city is square, and its length is as great as its width. He measured the city with the reed, twelve (12,012 stadia = 2,221 kilometers or 1,380 miles.)[13]. Its length, width, and height are equal.

What is the shape of the city?

What is the length and width of the city?

What is the height of the city?

Prayer: Again Father, our imagination boggles at the size of this city. Not only is the area equal to a large country, but the volume is like that of a moon. We cannot picture it, so we know You designed it to exceed our imaginations. Glory to You forever. Amen!

Its length, width, and height are equal. Thus, the future Jerusalem is like the Holy of Holies in the temple and the tabernacle, which were perfect cubes. God does not provide details about the interior of the city, whether there are multiple levels or not, but it doesn't matter. It will be awe-inspiring.

November 30 – Revelation 21:17

Its wall is one hundred forty-four cubits, (144 cubits is about 65.8 meters or 216 feet.)[13] by the measure of a man, that is, of an angel.

How tall was the wall?

How much of the city can be seen from outside the wall?

Prayer: Thank You, Father, for describing Your eternal city in so much detail. The clearer and more concrete You make it, the better is captures our imagination. Help us to dwell on our eternal future with You and not on our selfish interests. In Jesus's Name, we pray. Amen.

Its wall is one hundred forty-four cubits. Although this is a huge wall, it is minuscule compared to the gigantic city behind it. Thus, most of the city is visible to those outside the wall and to the rest of the dwellers on the new Earth.

December 1 – Revelation 21:18

The construction of its wall was jasper. The city was pure gold, like pure glass.

What was the wall made of?

What was the city made of?

Where do we frequently see gold and diamonds (jasper) paired together?

Prayer: Father, it is beyond belief that You are our wedding gift. Just as a precious jewel given from a husband to a bride, so You give new Jerusalem, with You and the Lamb dwelling in it as our eternal home. This alone is enough for us. Thank You. Amen.

The construction of its wall was jasper. The use of "jasper" is confusing for the modern definition does not align with the Biblical description. *Smith's Bible Dictionary* says:

Jasper — a precious stone frequently noticed in Scripture . It was the last of the twelve inserted in the high priest's breastplate (See **Exodus 28:20; 39:13**.) and the first of the twelve used in the foundations of the new Jerusalem. (See **Revelation 21:19**.) The characteristics of the stone as far as they are specified in Scripture (See **Revelation 21:11**.) are that it "was most precious" and "like crystal;" we may also infer (See **Revelation 4:3**.) that it was a stone of brilliant and transparent light. The stone which we name "jasper" does not accord with this description. There can be no doubt that the diamond would more adequately answer the description in the book of Revelation.[10]

December 2 – Revelation 21:19

The foundations of the city's wall were adorned with all kinds of precious stones. The first foundation was jasper; the second, sapphire; the third, chalcedony; the fourth, emerald.

What color is jasper?

What color is sapphire?

What color is chalcedony?

What color is emerald?

Prayer: Who else, O God, adorns a city's foundations with precious stones? Only You, Almighty One. With all wealth at Your disposal and perfect aesthetic sense, You know best how to bedeck Your city so its beauty best reflects Your glory. For You excel Your creation. Amen.

The first foundation was jasper. The city's wall has twelve foundations, with the first jasper or diamond. The bottom foundation links with the substance of the wall, and the remaining foundations each contribute a different color, rather like the stripes in the Grand Canyon. No mention is made of how tall the foundation is. It may double the height of the wall itself. All twelve foundations are visible from outside the city.

December 3 – Revelation 21:20

The fifth, sardonyx; the sixth, sardius; the seventh, chrysolite; the eighth, beryl; the ninth, topaz; the tenth, chrysoprase; the eleventh, jacinth; and the twelfth, amethyst.

What color is sardonyx?

What color is sardius?

What color is chrysolite?

What color is beryl?

What color is topaz?

What color is chrysoprase?

What color is jacinth?

What color is amethyst?

Prayer: Thank You, Lord God, for Your generosity. Not only do You give us precious gems, but You make them visible to all so that everyone may be delighted by the sight of Your city, reflecting Your glory forever. Amen.

And the twelfth, amethyst. Each gem is a different color, and the twelfth foundation is amethyst, a deep purple gem, the color of royalty. This is the color next to the jasper wall. Its purple color contrasts sharply with the glittering diamond above it.

December 4 - Revelation 21:21

The twelve gates were twelve pearls. Each one of the gates was made of one pearl. The street of the city was pure gold, like transparent glass.

What were the twelve gates made of?

What were the streets made of?

How can streets and gates made of these materials last for eternity?

Prayer: Father, You continue Your generosity to Your children, giving us gates of pearl to our capital city. Again, a pearl is perfect for reflecting and refracting all the glowing colors around it, so those who enter our city are delighted by rainbows of color. We praise You for Your extravagant love! Amen.

Each one of the gates was made of one pearl. One conception of these gates is a single, spherical pearl that fills a round portal in the wall. The glow from inside the city will stream out the twelve gates like twelve searchlights to the four corners of the new Earth.

December 5 – Revelation 21:22

I saw no temple in it, for the Lord God, the Almighty, and the Lamb, are its temple.

Where is the temple of the city?

How can God be a temple?

Prayer: O Father, You Yourself and the Lamb of God at Your side unify heaven and Earth in Your new creation. Having conquered sin and death, You now achieve Your goal of dwelling with mankind forever. All glory is Yours forever! Amen.

The Lord God, the Almighty, and the Lamb, are its temple. A temple is a place where man meets God, where heaven and Earth come together. Since God and the Lamb fill the city, the whole city is a temple, the holy of holies.

Consider the change: The holy of holies could only be entered once per year by the high priest. Now that the High Priest Jesus has paid for all the sins of all mankind, all may dwell with God forever.

December 6 – Revelation 21:23

The city has no need for the sun or moon to shine, for the very glory of God illuminated it, and its lamp is the Lamb.

What is the light of the city?

Does this mean the sun and moon no longer exist?

Does this mean the new Earth doesn't need to rotate?

Prayer: Father, You have said that no man knows the things You have prepared for us, yet our minds boggle at what You plan to do. We want to know how it will all work and look. Help us wait patiently for Your good and perfect gift. In Jesus's Name, we pray. Amen.

The very glory of God illuminated it, and its lamp is the Lamb. This is a striking image and the only time the Lamb is called a lamp. The Holy Spirit is pictured as a lamp, and Christians are pictured as having lamps and being lampstands. But here is a picture of Jesus Himself giving off the glory of God and illuminating the entire, planet-scale city.

December 7 – Revelation 21:24

The nations will walk in its light. The kings of the earth bring the glory and honor of the nations into it.

Who populates the city?

Who visits the city and brings gifts?

What does this imply about the rest of the new Earth?

Prayer: Father, You only give us the faintest hints of the rest of the Earth outside Your city. But what You show is glorious. All of mankind is saved and walking without sin while living on the Earth, just as You intended from the very beginning. Even so, come Lord Jesus! Amen.

The kings of the earth bring the glory and honor of the nations into it. There is much implied here. "The kings" indicates monarchal governments over the nations of Earth. "Bring their glory and honor" indicates gift giving of the highest sort. The best of each nation will pour into new Jerusalem, voluntarily, out of the love of these kings and the love of these nations for God. This also implies that the nations will abound in wealth so that each will have much to give.

December 8 – Revelation 21:25

Its gates will in no way be shut by day (for there will be no night there).

Will the gates ever be shut?

What does that say about access to God?

What does the lack of night say about the sleep cycles of the inhabitants?

Prayer: Father in heaven, You never slumber, never sleep, and You have limitless energy, and we always have access to You. We look forward to being filled with Your power and living a life without sleep, but full of meaning, with You. Amen.

For there will be no night there. God gave the night for rest.

Psalm 104:21-23 *You make darkness, and it is night, in which all the animals of the forest prowl.²² The sun rises, and they steal away, and lie down in their dens.²³ Man goes out to his work, to his labor until the evening.*

When we have our new spiritual bodies, we will be like Christ, and we will not need rest.

1 John 3:2 *Beloved, now we are children of God. It is not yet revealed what we will be; but we know that when he is revealed, we will be like him; for we will see him just as he is.*

December 9 – Revelation 21:26

And they shall bring the glory and the honor of the nations into it so that they may enter.

What comes into the city?

1.

2.

Who comes into the city?

Prayer: Father, we get the picture of kings and rulers entering Your capital of new Jerusalem all the time, bringing the glory and honor of their nation as gifts for You. You accept them and place them in Your city, making it ever more glorious with beauty from around the world. This way all the people of the world are invested in Your city and contribute to it. Glory to You forever! Amen.

So that they may enter. When the kings of the Earth come to new Jerusalem, they are coming before their King and must honor Him with their gift. I imagine there will be an effort to bring the best possible gift to God every time they visit Jesus.

December 10 – Revelation 21:27

There will in no way enter into it anything profane, or one who causes an abomination or a lie, but only those who are written in the Lamb's book of life.

Who is not in the city?

1.

2.

3.

Who is the city?

What does this say about the salvation of the rest of the Earth's inhabitants?

Prayer: Father, it seems impossible to us, yet You will create a universe without sin. All people will live without sinning and will not fear death, but instead look forward to glory with You. You give us severe warnings now to forsake sin. Help us to listen and do it! In Jesus's Name, we pray. Amen.

But only those who are written in the Lamb's book of life – The Book of Life is covered in the appendix. Those who were not in the Book of Life were previously cast into the lake of fire. (See **Revelation 20:15.**)

December 11 - Revelation 22:1

He showed me a river of water of life, clear as crystal, proceeding out of the throne of God and of the Lamb.

What is in the city?

Where does the river originate?

Where else does a river appear in a dwelling of God and man?

Prayer: O Lord Jesus Christ, You promised rivers of living water, and here you fulfill Your promise, giving living water to all mankind. Glory to You forever, for giving us eternal life through the Holy Spirit! Amen.

Proceeding out of the throne of God and of the Lamb. Although there is no temple in the city, God has His throne there, and the river of the water of life issues from it. This is also pictured in Ezekiel:

Ezekiel 47:1-5 *He brought me back to the door of the house; and behold, waters flowed out from under the threshold of the house eastward, for the front of the house faced toward the east. The waters came down from underneath, from the right side of the house, on the south of the altar.[2] Then he brought me out by the way of the gate northward, and led me around by the way outside to the outer gate, by the way of the gate that looks toward the east. Behold, waters ran out on the right side.[3] When the man went out eastward with the line in his hand, he measured one thousand cubits and he caused me to pass through the waters, waters that were to the ankles.[4] Again he measured one thousand, and caused me to pass through the waters, waters that were to the knees. Again he measured one thousand, and caused me to pass through waters that were to the waist.[5] Afterward he measured one thousand; and it was a river that I could not pass through; for the waters had risen, waters to swim in, a river that could not be walked through.*

And in **Zechariah 14:8** *It will happen in that day, that living waters will go out from Jerusalem: half of them toward the eastern sea, and half of them toward the western sea.*

December 12 – Revelation 22:2

…in the middle of its street. On this side of the river and on that was the tree of life, bearing twelve kinds of fruits, yielding its fruit every month. The leaves of the tree were for the healing of the nations.

Where was the river?

What was on the sides of the river?

What did the tree of life bear?

How often did it bear fruit?

What else did it supply?

Prayer: O Lord God, Your city has been copied by men. We have many streets with broad green areas in the middle of the street. But Your conception surpasses them all. We will stroll down the streets, be able to eat the fruit and drink the water at any time, and be refreshed with eternal life. Praise to You forever! Amen.

The tree of life, bearing twelve kinds of fruits, yielding its fruit every month. In the middle of the city, there will be a variety of fruit and flowers on these trees of life. The flowers are implied. Likely, there will be different flowers each month in preparation for next month's fruit.

—

December 13 – Revelation 22:3

There will be no curse any more. The throne of God and of the Lamb will be in it, and his servants will serve him.

Is this end of all curses for new Jerusalem, the Earth, or all of the new heavens and new Earth? Why do you think so?

Who is in the city?

What shall b**e done in the city?**

Prayer: Father, thank You for training us now to serve Jesus Christ, so that we may serve You for all eternity with joy and fulfillment. Glory to God forever! Amen.

The throne of God and of the Lamb will be in it. One might wonder, "Where is the Holy Spirit?" The Holy Spirit has been mentioned symbolically by the River of Life, coming from the throne of God. His Spirit goes out from God and changes the universe as He pleases.

–

December 14 – Revelation 22:4

They will see his face, and his name will be on their foreheads.

What honor do the servants of God have?

How close will His servants come to God?

How close will God be to them?

Prayer: Father, Your Revelation through Jesus makes us exercise our imagination. This may be the hardest for us to picture: Your face gazing upon us with love, and Your Name upon us forever. Thank You, in the Name of Jesus. Amen.

His name will be on their foreheads. Now we are called "Christians" and "children of God," so God's name is now upon Christians. But then, Christ's name may be visible to all.

–

December 15 – Revelation 22:5

There will be no night, and they need no lamp light or sun light; for the Lord God will illuminate them. They will reign forever and ever.

What is the light of the city?

How long will God's servants reign?

Prayer: Father, just as You provided the sun to shine by day and the moon by night, they will no longer be necessary in Your Presence in the city of God. You are our sun and moon, our Light of the world. Thank you, Jesus! Amen.

They will reign forever and ever. This is significant, for the reigning of God's children continues without end. The rule over the Earth from Jesus's return until the white throne judgment is clear, (See **Revelation 20:11-13** for details about the judgment.) but this reign continues into the new heavens and the new Earth. The details of the subjects and the territory are not covered.

–

December 16 – Revelation 22:6

He said to me, "These words are faithful and true. The Lord God of the spirits of the prophets sent his angel to show to his bondservants the things which must happen soon."

Who sent the angel?

To whom was the angel sent?

When shall these things come to pass?

Prayer: Father, although You say "soon," it seems like a long time from John's day to now to us. But two thousand years is nothing to You. Help us to wait patiently and faithfully for Jesus to come. Amen.

"These words are faithful and true." The angel refers to himself modestly in the third person, but he testifies his words are true since they come from God Himself, the same God who spoke by the prophets of the Old Testament.

–

December 17 – Revelation 22:7

"Behold, I come quickly. Blessed is he who keeps the words of the prophecy of this book."

Who is speaking?

What is His promise?

What is His blessing?

Prayer: Lord Jesus Christ, You're still speaking to us who read the book of Revelation. You're still blessing those who read and keep the words of the book. Help us so we never fail You. Let us still be busy doing Your work when You return. Amen.

"Behold, I come quickly." John probably wrote this around 90 AD, nearly two thousand years ago. This doesn't seem "quick" to us, but God's perspective is different. Whether you compare this time to the thousands of years humanity was on the Earth or to the billions since creation, this is a short time.

–

December 18 – Revelation 22:8

Now I, John, am the one who heard and saw these things. When I heard and saw, I fell down to worship before the feet of the angel who had shown me these things.

What was John's reaction to the revelation?

Why did he react this way?

Prayer: Father, we are so human. We tend to praise or curse the messenger for good or bad news or worship them if they carry a message from You. We can only sympathize with John in this unique situation and pray that we keep our eyes on You and not the messenger You may use. Amen.

I fell down to worship before the feet of the angel. This is the second time John attempted to worship an angel.

Revelation 19:10 *I fell down before his feet to worship him. He said to me, "Look! Don't do it! I am a fellow bondservant with you and with your brothers who hold the testimony of Jesus. Worship God, for the testimony of Jesus is the Spirit of Prophecy."*

—

December 19 – Revelation 22:9

He said to me, "See you don't do it! I am a fellow bondservant with you and with your brothers, the prophets, and with those who keep the words of this book. Worship God."

What are the angel's commands?

1.

2.

To whom does the angel speak?

Prayer: Father, we're sorry we don't listen to Your Word the first time, nor do we immediately obey You. Be patient with us, even as You were with Your servant John. In the Name of the Spirit of Prophecy, we pray. Amen

"I am a fellow bondservant with you and with your brothers, the prophets, and with those who keep the words of this book." The angel, the one who carried one of the last plagues, puts himself as equal with John's fellow Christians and the prophets. He also equates himself with all servants of God who read and keep the words of the book of Revelation.

–

December 20 – Revelation 22:10

He said to me, "Don't seal up the words of the prophecy of this book, for the time is at hand."

What is the angel's instruction?

To whom is he speaking?

Why does the angel say this?

Prayer: Father, ever since Peter's first sermon in **Acts 2** we know we have been in the end days. Let us not grow weary of doing Your work in our lives. Let us press on and sprint to the finish line where we will meet You. In Jesus's Name, we pray. Amen.

"Don't seal up the words of the prophecy of this book." This is in contrast with the end of the book of Daniel where the angel says:

Daniel 12:9 *He said, "Go your way, Daniel; for the words are shut up and sealed until the time of the end."*

–

December 21 – Revelation 22:11

"He who acts unjustly, let him act unjustly still. He who is filthy, let him be filthy still. He who is righteous, let him do righteousness still. He who is holy, let him be holy still."

What does the angel say?

1.

2.

3.

4.

What does this mean?

Prayer: Holy God, before we know it, we'll be out of time. Help us to repent now. Help us do righteousness now. Help us to be holy now. Help us to always be faithful to You, no matter how much time we have left. In the Name of the Word of God, we pray. Amen.

"He who acts unjustly, let him act unjustly still." The fearful implication of these words is that the time is up for repentance. That time is not in John's day, nor in our day, but some day there will be no time left to repent. At that point, the wicked's fate will be decided.

—

December 22 – Revelation 22:12

"Behold, I come quickly. My reward is with me, to repay to each man according to his work."

Who is speaking?

What does He promise?

1.

2.

How does He reward every man?

Prayer: Father, although eternal life is a gift from You, our reward depends upon our work. Help us to work according to Your will for the rest of our lives without wearying. In the Name of the Lamb of God, we pray. Amen.

"My reward is with me, to repay to each man according to his work." Jesus talks much about giving rewards in the gospel:

Luke 6:35 *But love your enemies, and do good, and lend, expecting nothing back; and your reward will be great, and you will be children of the Most High; for he is kind toward the unthankful and evil.*

Matthew 25:21 *"His lord said to him, 'Well done, good and faithful servant. You have been faithful over a few things, I will set you over many things. Enter into the joy of your lord.'"*

Matthew 25:34-36 *"Then the King will tell those on his right hand, 'Come, blessed of my Father, inherit the Kingdom prepared for you from the foundation of the world;[35] for I was hungry and you gave me food to eat. I was thirsty and you gave me drink. I was a stranger and you took me in.[36] I was naked and you clothed me. I was sick and you visited me. I was in prison and you came to me.'"*

December 23 – Revelation 22:13

"I am the Alpha and the Omega, the First and the Last, the Beginning and the End."

Who is speaking?

What names does He call Himself?

Why does He choose these names here, in the last chapter of the Bible?

Prayer: My Lord Jesus, You have an infinite number of names, for Your infinite attributes. Help us right now to remember that You have been here from the beginning, that You see into the infinite future, and to trust You in everything. Amen.

"The Alpha and the Omega." Jesus begins His six names in this verse with the first and the last letters of the Greek alphabet. We'd say, "I'm the A and Z." By this, He shows He encompasses all time, all creation, and all of the Bible. He was in **Genesis 1:1** and is at the end of Revelation.

December 24 – Revelation 22:14

Blessed are those who do his commandments, that they may have the right to the tree of life, and may enter in by the gates into the city.

Who is blessed?

What is the blessing?

1.

2.

How many of mankind receive this blessing in the new heavens and new Earth?

Prayer: Father, in this unimaginable future, everyone will live forever, with no death. There will be no crime and no harm, but all will achieve their full potential as human beings and children of God. Help us to bring this good news to everyone! Amen.

Blessed are those who do his commandments. Since there is no death, there is no sin. Without sin, everyone keeps God's commands. And blessings unmeasured fall upon humanity and all creation.

December 25 – Revelation 22:15

Outside are the dogs, the sorcerers, the sexually immoral, the murderers, the idolaters, and everyone who loves and practices falsehood.

Who are outside the city?

1.

2.

3.

4.

5.

Prayer: Lord God Almighty, we often underestimate our sin, thinking the little lie or selfish act doesn't matter. But all sin separates us from You and eternal life with You. Help us to reconcile with You now, while we can, through our Lord and Savior, Jesus Christ, who died for all our sins. In His Name, Amen.

Everyone who loves and practices falsehood. This sin list covers the major categories of sin we commit and closes with lying, which is our most common and frequent sin. We like to rank sin in tiers, but all sin is hateful to God, Who only deals in truth.

December 26 – Revelation 22:16

"I, Jesus, have sent my angel to testify these things to you for the assemblies. I am the root and the offspring of David, the Bright and Morning Star."

What is Jesus's testimony?

How does Jesus name Himself?

1.

2.

To whom does Jesus testify these things?

Prayer: Father, here we are, in Your churches on the Earth. Help us to think about and live these lessons in our lives. Help everyone to do these things, beginning today. In the Name of the Sun of Righteousness, we pray. Amen.

"I, Jesus, have sent my angel to testify these things to you for the assemblies." "These things" refers to the whole book of Revelation. Since this book ends the Bible, it could also be taken as referring to the whole Bible. "Angel" means messenger and can refer to one from heaven or a person on Earth bearing His message.

December 27 – Revelation 22:17

The Spirit and the bride say, "Come!" He who hears, let him say, "Come!" He who is thirsty, let him come. He who desires, let him take the water of life freely.

What is the invitation?

1.

2.

Who makes the invitation?

1.

2.

3.

To whom is this invitation?

Prayer: Father, You cannot be more open, more inviting to mankind than You are. You freely offer eternal life to all, through Your Son Jesus Christ. You will pour out Your Spirit of eternal life upon all who come and are saved. We praise You forever. Amen.

The Spirit and the bride say, "Come!" The Spirit and the bride begin the holy invitation. Each person may come as they hear the truth from the Church and are moved by the Spirit. Then those who thirst for something more are urged to invite others to the water of life. Finally, anyone who desires eternal life may freely drink.

December 28 – Revelation 22:18

I testify to everyone who hears the words of the prophecy of this book, if anyone adds to them, may God add to him the plagues which are written in this book.

Who is warned of a curse?

What curse is pronounced?

Who receives this curse?

Prayer: Ah, Lord God, let us greatly fear to take away any words of the book and to add any words to it. You are serious, and Your Word is serious. Let us also be serious as we read and seek to understand. In the name of the Word of God, we pray. Amen.

I testify to everyone who hears the words of the prophecy of this book. Jesus uses "hear" because most of the time letters and books of the Bible were read aloud in the congregation. Private, personal copies were rare or nonexistent.

December 29 – Revelation 22:19

If anyone takes away from the words of the book of this prophecy, may God take away his part from the tree of life, and out of the holy city, which are written in this book.

What is the last curse in the Bible?

Who receives this curse?

What do these people lose?

Prayer: Lord Jesus, let us cling to our part of the tree of life and not reject You by rejecting Your Word. Help us to fear and to obey! Amen.

May God take away his part from the tree of life. God did this to Adam and Eve when they sinned, and they died, as did all their children. Thus began our era of death and sin. Now God is reversing this and calling people to His tree of life. But those who delete the message will be deleted from life.

December 30 – Revelation 22:20

He who testifies these things says, "Yes, I come quickly." Amen! Yes, come, Lord Jesus.

Who is speaking?

What is the last promise of Jesus?

Who says, "Yes, come, Lord Jesus"?

Prayer: Father, we need to wait patiently for Jesus's quick return. Help us with our patience. Let us not look to our perception of time but to Your perspective. Help us redeem our time wisely, doing Your work and Your will. In Jesus's Name, we pray. Amen.

Amen! Yes, come, Lord Jesus. This exclamation probably burst from John's heart as he wrote these last few verses.

December 31 – Revelation 22:21

The grace of the Lord Jesus Christ be with all the saints. Amen.

What is the last statement of the Bible?

Who is it addressed to?

Why do you think Jesus inspired John to end the book this way?

Prayer: Father, You leave us with a vision of the infinite future and sufficient grace for our salvation in this time, wherever we are, whenever we read this book. Help us to live in the grace of Jesus Christ and give that grace to everyone we meet. In the name of our Lord of grace, we pray. Amen.

The grace of the Lord Jesus Christ be with all the saints. Amen. Amen.

Bibliography

1. - *Asbury Bible Commentary*, Copyright © 1992 by The Zondervan Corporation. Biblegateway.com

2. - *Bible Panorama* Copyright © 2005 Day One Publications, Biblegateway.com

3. - *IVP New Testament Commentary Series*, IVP New Testament Commentaries are made available by the generosity of InterVarsity Press., Biblegateway.com

4. - Got Questions? "What are Jachin and Boaz?", https://www.gotquestions.org/Jachin-and-Boaz.html

5. - Keller, Timothy and Kathy, *The Songs of Jesus*, (Viking Press, November 2015)

6. - *Matthew Henry's Commentary*, Biblegateway.com

7. - Miller, CDS, from Wikileaks, A Map of Megido, https://starlogic.ca/2020/04/29/wikileaks-dump-had-a-map-of-megiddo/comment-page-1/?unapproved=7550&moderation-hash=49d6860e53abf07abc93cc36fcb85afd#comment-7550

8. - Minimum wage, US, https://www.dol.gov/agencies/whd/mw-consolidated

9. - Learn Religions, Fairchild, Mary, "How Heavy Was a Talent in the Bible?", https://www.learnreligions.com/what-is-a-talent-700699

10. - Smith's Bible Dictionary, " Jasper", https://biblehub.com/topical/j/jasper.html

11. - Smith, Jeffry, *The Gospel Medley*, (Peoria Illinois, Jule Inc, 2021)

12. - *Twenty-Six Translations of the Bible, Volume 3* (Grand Rapids: The Zondervan Corporation, 1985).

13. - *World English Bible* (WEB) by Public Domain. The name

"World English Bible" is trademarked. From Biblegateway.com

14. - Wheat, prices of in the US, https://www.selinawamucii.com/insights/prices/united-states-of-america/wheat/

15. - Wikipedia, "Laodecia on the Lycus", https://en.wikipedia.org/wiki/Laodicea_on_the_Lycus

16. - *The Zondervan Parallel New Testament in Greek and English* (Grand Rapids: Zondervan Bible Publishers, 1980).

17. - Wikipedia: Number of the beast, https://en.wikipedia.org/wiki/Number_of_the_beast, From footnote 31: Pate, C. Marvin; Haines, Calvin B. (1995). Doomsday delusions: what's wrong with predictions about the end of the world. Downers Grove, IL: InterVarsity Press. pp. 41–42. ISBN 978-0-8308-1621-7.

Appendix — The Book of Life

The Book of Life is a profound topic. This is a Scripture survey of the topic using "book of life" and "your book" as my search elements. I summarize each verse.

Exodus 32:32-33 *Yet now, if you will, forgive their sin — and if not, please blot me out of your book which you have written."*[33] *Yahweh said to Moses, "Whoever has sinned against me, I will blot him out of my book.*

- Moses was in the Book of Life, and he knew it.
- Moses knew the LORD God wrote the Book of Life.
- Moses knew names could be blotted from God's Book of Life.
- The Lord Yahweh can blot out names from the Book of Life.
- God blots out the names of those who sin against Him.

Psalm 40:7-8 *Then I said, "Behold, I have come. It is written about me in the book in the scroll.*[8] *I delight to do your will, my God. Yes, your law is within my heart."*

- David says that his coming to God and delight in God is written in the book.

Psalm 56:8 *You count my wanderings. You put my tears into your container. Aren't they in your book?*

- All our tears and wanderings are in the Book of Life.

Psalm 69:19-28 *You know my reproach, my shame, and my dishonor. My adversaries are all before you.*[20] *Reproach has broken my heart, and I am full of heaviness. I looked for some to take pity, but there was none; for comforters, but I found none.*

21 They also gave me poison for my food. In my thirst, they gave me vinegar to drink.
22 Let their table before them become a snare. May it become a retribution and a trap.
23 Let their eyes be darkened, so that they can't see. Let their backs be

continually bent. 24 Pour out your indignation on them. Let the fierceness of your anger overtake them.

25 Let their habitation be desolate. Let no one dwell in their tents. 26 For they persecute him whom you have wounded. They tell of the sorrow of those whom you have hurt.

27 Charge them with crime upon crime. Don't let them come into your righteousness.

28 Let them be blotted out of the book of life, and not be written with the righteous.

- David prayed that his merciless and unjust adversaries would be blotted out of God's Book of Life.
- David knew God had that power.
- The righteous are in the Book of Life

Psalm 139:15-16 *My frame wasn't hidden from you, when I was made in secret, woven together in the depths of the earth. 16 Your eyes saw my body. In your book they were all written, the days that were ordained for me, when as yet there were none of them.*

- Our body is described in the Book of Life.
- Our whole life is in it.
- This was written before we were born.

Daniel 12:1 *"At that time Michael will stand up, the great prince who stands for the children of your people; and there will be a time of trouble, such as never was since there was a nation even to that same time. At that time your people will be delivered, everyone who is found written in the book."*

- Those written in the Book of Life are delivered from the time of trouble at the end.

Philippians 4:3 *Yes, I beg you also, true partner, help these women, for they labored with me in the Good News with Clement also, and the rest of my fellow workers, whose names are in the book of life.*

- Christians' names are in the Book of Life.

Revelation 3:5 *He who overcomes will be arrayed in white garments, and I will in no way blot his name out of the book of life, and I will confess his name before my Father, and before his angels.*

- Jesus does not blot out the names of overcomers from the Book of Life.
- This implies Jesus can blot names from the Book of Life.

Revelation 13:8 *All who dwell on the earth will worship him, everyone whose name has not been written from the foundation of the world in the book of life of the Lamb who has been killed.*

- Those who worship the beast do not have their names written in the Book of Life.
- The Book of Life is written at the foundation of the world.

Revelation 17:8 *The beast that you saw was, and is not; and is about to come up out of the abyss and to go into destruction. Those who dwell on the earth and whose names have not been written in the book of life from the foundation of the world will marvel when they see that the beast was, and is not, and shall be present.*

- Those who marvel at the beast do not have their names written in the Book of Life.

Revelation 20:12 *I saw the dead, the great and the small, standing before the throne, and they opened books. Another book was opened, which is the book of life. The dead were judged out of the things which were written in the books, according to their works.*

Revelation 20:15 *If anyone was not found written in the book of life, he was cast into the lake of fire.*

Revelation 21:27 *There will in no way enter into it anything profane, or one who causes an abomination or a lie, but only those who are written in the Lamb's book of life.*

- Those who are not in the Book of Life are cast into the lake of fire at the white throne judgment.
- Those who are profane, and unholy, causing abominations and lies are not written in the Book of Life.

What is not said

- Who writes the names in the Book of life? God does, but does the Father or Son or both?
- When God blots out a person's name from the Book of Life is not clear. Is it during their lifetime?

What is implied?

My viewpoint:
- When Jesus blots out people's names from the Book of Life, it is while they are still living.
- These people's names were in the Book of Life from the foundation of the world but were removed by Jesus's judgment during their lifetime.

Acknowledgements

I could not have completed this book without the efforts of my editors Leslie McKie and Rik Hall. They led me to countless corrections and improvements.

My illustrator Pat Marvenko Smith and my cover designer Sean Flanagan did great work in capturing the striking images from Revelation and making a captivating book cover.

Also, I must thank my Revelation class Bible students at Northwoods Community Church. Their questions and insights honed my own perspective of Revelation and gave me greater understanding of the book.

Biography

Born and reared in Cleveland, Ohio, Jeffry grew up with a lively interest in dinosaurs, outer space, and all things scientific. Upon learning the meaning of "agnostic" at age eight, he applied that to himself. However, at age twelve, while investigating cosmology and its related theories, he realized God had to exist for the universe to come from nothing. He then converted to Christianity and began a lifelong study of the Bible.

During his career in information technology and process improvement, Jeffry began a study of Revelation where he wrote down every statement in the book. Later, he converted that study into an inductive study of Revelation, which he taught at his church.

After publishing *The Gospel Medley,* Jeffry decided to convert his Revelation study into a daily devotional on the book of Revelation.

Jeffry has also written eight fiction books under the pen name Andy Zach.

Jeffry is now retired and writes full-time. He lives with his wife and children in Peoria, Illinois.

Index